Dedication

This book is dedicated to the more than two million Americans who are behind bars.

In addition, the book is dedicated to the untold number of fellow-citizens who, though not behind bars, seek an expanded degree of personal freedom in their own lives.

Acknowledgements

First, appreciation is extended to the sixteen prison mentors whose stories appear in this book. Thanks for the personal courage of their lives and for telling their stories so honestly.

Thanks to the dozens of inmates at the Utah State Prison I became acquainted with and who inspired me to become involved in a worthy cause.

In the production of this book, extraordinary thanks and appreciation is expressed to Melissa Stevens who added enormously to the message of the book by superbly creating drawings of the sixteen mentors.

For proofreading and suggestions, appreciation is expressed to Carol Lynn Pearson, Marie Cheever Surnovszky, David Wright, and Warren Wright. Thanks to the staff at CreateSpace in producing the book.

Special appreciation and thanks is given to my wife Susie who supported my writing efforts with constant encouragement and optimism.

Author Biography

Donald L. Wright, PhD, is a writer, humanitarian, and a public school system retiree. He has traveled the world, from Hawaii, to Italy, to Saudi Arabia, and Hong Kong, but it was one night spent in a Mexican jail cell that had the most influence on the rest of his life. He went on to serve five-years at the Utah State Prison, this time as a volunteer.

While teaching courses in prison and facilitating college classes, he grew to know hundreds of inmates, as well as their personal stories and many of their concerns.

Wright then established the PrisonEd Foundation to fill the critical need for educational opportunities for the incarcerated.

Freedom Behind Bars is his second book, following *Beside Still Waters: 52 Reflections of the Divine Within*. He lives in Sandy, Utah with his wife. Together, they have five children and eleven grandchildren.

Contents

1

The Mind-Forged Manacles

My first involvement with jail was when I was a college student on Christmas break. Two friends and I drove to Mexico. We had little money, and in Acapulco we slept in our old Volkswagen van in a farmer's field. We spent the next morning on the beach, and as we started to get in the car a half-dozen police officers hauled us to jail, accusing us of stealing money from a hotel. The best Spanish I could come up with was, "Senor, amigo, amigo, we bueno hombres, we no banditos!" No luck. We were locked in three separate cells in our swim suits.

Looking through the bars, I watched the sun go down. I was hungry, and with the setting of the sun it began to get cold. I had no idea how long we would be held. I thought a lot about the things I wanted to do with my life. Late that night, in the dark, we were released. When we got back to our car we found that it had been broken into and my wallet and sixty dollars were gone. I vowed to avoid jails in the future.

However, many years later, I served a five-year sentence at the Utah State Prison. Happily, I was there as a volunteer. I became acquainted with more than a hundred inmates and with many of their concerns.

THE MIND-FORGED MANACLES

I was reminded of a poem by William Blake. Note the memorable last line.

> I wander thro' each charter'd street,
> Near where the charter'd Thames does flow,
> And mark in ever face I meet
> Marks of weakness, marks of woe.
> In every cry of every Man,
> In every Infant's cry of fear
> In every voice, in every ban,
> The mind-forg'd manacles I hear.[1]

Such an intriguing phrase – *the mind-forg'd manacles*. Whether one is incarcerated or not, these manacles are the chains we place on ourselves or allow others to place on us, or perhaps they just show up. They may be an obsession in meeting the expectations of others, diminished expectations of self, or accepting a mentality of scarcity. The mind-forged manacles may be a prison of drugs or alcohol. They may be a prison without love, nurturing or encouragement. They may be a prison of self-indulgence without concern for others. They may be a prison of meaninglessness, of only being an actor performing someone else's lines. The result is like trying to play a trombone in a telephone booth.

Albert Einstein spoke of a prison of the mind as he noticed a common narrowness in people, which he referred to as a delusion.

> This delusion is a kind of *prison* for us, restricting us to
> our personal desires and to affection for a few persons
> nearest us. Our task must be to free ourselves from this
> *prison* by widening our circles of compassion to embrace

all living creatures and the whole of nature in its beauty.[2] (italics added)

> The artist Vincent van Gogh saw himself as one of the *prisoners* in an I-don't-know-what-for horrible, horrible, utterly horrible cage . . . I know that I might be a totally different man! How then can I be useful, how can I be of service! Something is alive in me: what can it be![3] (italics added)

David, king of Israel, when confined by his enemies to a cave, cried to God, "Bring my *soul* out of *prison*."[4] (italics added)

It appears there are many whose soul is in prison – whether incarcerated or not. Many may not even notice because demands, trivia, and hurry crowd out introspection. It is easy to grow used to the status quo, even when the quo has lost its status.

FREEDOM BEHIND BARS

Those behind bars have two release dates to schedule – one from the prison behind bars, and two from the prison of the mind. John, an inmate friend, told me, "I have filled my heart with happiness . . . I never would have guessed that such gorgeous freedom was available right here in prison." Bill Dallas, whose story is told in this book, made this observation regarding some of the "lifers" at San Quentin. "[They] lacked physical freedom but had achieved personal freedom in their minds, hearts, and spirits. The fact that they were behind bars was irrelevant."

An English prisoner, Richard Lovelace, wrote of his freedom in the poem, "To Althea from Prison," including these last lines:

> Stone walls do not a prison make, Nor iron bars a cage;
> Minds innocent and quiet take that for an Hermitage;
> If I have freedom in my love, And in my soul am free;
> Angels alone that soar above Enjoy such liberty.[5]

While many prisoners I knew were merely *doing* time, others *embraced* time. Fascinated, I began reading biographies of prisoners who escaped the mind-forged manacles and found an astonishing degree of freedom behind cement walls and steel bars.

I discovered there are some who successfully go through the crucible of prison and acquire an exceptional depth of character. I found their stories fascinating. The next chapters introduce you to sixteen remarkable individuals who have served time in prison. They are men and women who used their prison experience as a springboard for exhilarating adventures of discovery.

These sixteen prisoners have taught me memorable lessons about personal freedom. They are my *mentors from prison*. I am delighted to introduce you – no matter which side of the bars you are on.

"I came out mature"

2
Nelson Mandela
1918 - 2013

Nelson Mandela was sentenced to life imprisonment at age 44. He spent 27 years in prison and was released at age 71. He was elected the first black president of South Africa at age 75 and fused an apartheid nation on the brink of a civil war into the "Rainbow Nation." Mandela was asked the question, how did the man who emerged from prison differ from the willful young man who entered it? He replied, "I came out mature."

EARLY LIFE

Nelson Mandela wrote a large part of his autobiography in prison, aptly titled, *Long Walk to Freedom*.[1] He was born July 18, 1918 and was given the name Rolihlaha (which means "troublemaker). "On the first day of school my teacher, Miss Mdingane, gave each of us an English name . . . . [She] told me that my new name was Nelson. Why this particular name I have no idea."

When Mandela was nine, his father died of tuberculosis. Mandela went to live with a relative who was a local chief. In college, he was involved in a boycott against the quality of food and was temporarily suspended. He left school without receiving a degree. Back home, he found the chief had arranged a marriage for him, and he fled to Johannesburg. He worked as a law-firm clerk and took correspondence courses to complete his B.A. "Many days I walked the six miles to town in the morning and the six back in the evening in order to save bus fare. I often went days without more than a mouthful of food and without a change of clothing."

Mandela was frustrated with the racism that was rampant in South Africa. He protested conditions and was arrested several times on various charges of sabotage, insurrection, conspiracy, and high treason. After lengthy trials, finally he was convicted and sentenced to life imprisonment.

PRISON AT ROBBEN ISLAND

Mandela spent the first 18 years of his incarceration at Robben Island in a damp, concrete cell 7 feet by 8 feet. He reported, "It never seemed to go above forty degrees Fahrenheit." He slept on a straw mat, had three ragged blankets, was required to wear short pants, and wore shoes without socks. Of the food he said, "The authorities liked to say that we received a balanced diet; it was indeed balanced – between the unpalatable and the inedible." He washed with a bucket of cold sea water. For sixteen years he had no access to newspapers or radio. "We were only permitted to write to our immediate families, and just one letter of five hundred words every six months."[2] Letters, when they came, were often delayed for long periods and made unreadable by the prison censors.

> Each morning, a load of stones about the size of volleyballs was dumped by the entrance to the courtyard. Using wheelbarrows, we moved the stones to the center of the yard . . . . Our job was to crush the stones into gravel . . . . The work was tedious and difficult.[3]

For thirteen years he mined lime. The never-ending task was to chop huge blocks of limestone from the earth, wrestle them to the road, beat them into gravel or powder, and cart it all away.

With all the regulations of prison life, Mandela still maintained his own personal discipline. Rising before dawn, "I would do stationary running in my cell . . . for up to forty-five minutes. I would also perform one hundred fingertip push-ups, two hundred sit-ups, fifty deep knee-bends, and various other calisthenics."[4] At night, through a correspondence program, he worked on a law degree. In addition, he began writing his autobiography, smuggling pages to London. When this activity was discovered, his study privileges for his law degree were stopped for four years. As a youth, Mandela had been baptized into the Methodist faith. During his 27 years in prison he missed only one Sunday church service and that was from illness.

Mandela gained deep respect for his fellow inmates. "[They were] men of such extraordinary courage, wisdom, and generosity that their like may never be known again. Perhaps it requires such depth of oppression to create such heights of character."[5] When Mandela became president, he appointed one of his fellow prisoners to be the minister of prisons – becoming the boss of his former guards.

Mandela found compassion for the guards.

> No one is born hating another person because of the color of his skin, or his background, or his religion. People must learn to hate, and if they can learn to hate, they can be taught to love, for love comes more naturally to the human heart than its opposite. Even in the grimmest times in prison, when my comrades and I were pushed to our limits, I would see a glimmer of humanity in one of the guards, perhaps just for a second, but it was enough to reassure me and keep me going. Man's goodness is a flame that can be hidden but never extinguished.[6]

"I never seriously considered the possibility that I would not emerge from prison one day. I never thought that a life sentence truly meant life and that I would die behind bars." This attitude prompted Mandela to use incarceration to prepare for his after-prison mission. He learned to speak Afrikaans. He learned the history of the Dutch oppressors, and he learned their game of rugby. In the next paragraph, he describes one of his proudest achievements.

> In the struggle, Robben Island was known as the University. This is not only because of what we learned from books, or because prisoners studied English, Afrikaans, art, geography, and mathematics, or because so many of our men . . . earned multiple degrees. Robben Island was known as the university because of what we learned from each other. We became our own faculty, with our own professors, our own curriculum, our own courses.[7]

RELEASE AND POLITICS

Even during his incarceration, Mandela was regarded as a leader of the black people of South Africa. The government understood the real possibility of civil war between blacks and whites. Those governing also saw the possibility that Mandela could be a key in working out a peaceful solution. He was transferred to prisons closer to Cape Town where prison conditions were significantly improved. Government officials began secret talks with him. After 27 years, at age 71, Nelson Mandela was released from prison. He was free to pursue his mission.

> I saw that it was not just my freedom that was curtailed, but the freedom of everyone who looked like I did . . . that is when the hunger for my own freedom became the greater hunger for the freedom of my people. It was this desire for the freedom of my people to live their lives with dignity and self-respect that animated my life, that transformed a frightened young man into a bold one. . . . When I walked out of prison that was my mission, to liberate the oppressed and the oppressor both.[8]

Though the political situation was unstable and precarious, a national election was agreed upon with black votes counting equally with white votes. Mandela was elected president of the African National Congress (ANC) and was their candidate for president. The following story illustrates both the volatile nature of the campaign and Mandela's diplomacy.

> Mandela went on a nighttime talk show to answer caller questions live. Eddie von Maltitz, a far-right warrior, blasted Mandela for 3 minutes including a brutally direct threat. After a tense pause, Mandela replied, 'Well, Eddie, I regard you as a worthy South African and I have no doubt that if we were to sit down and exchange views I will come closer to you and you will come closer to me. Let's talk, Eddie.' 'Uh…Right, okay, Mr. Mandela, Thank you,' and he hung up.[9]

Three months later Eddie had stopped his preparations for war saying, "The exchange on Radio 702 had changed everything. That was what got me thinking."

PRESIDENT OF SOUTH AFRICA

The country voted, and at age 75 Nelson Mandela won 62 percent of the national vote becoming president of the nation of South Africa. His task was daunting. Neither side trusted the other. Elements of the white population were fearful they would be oppressed and some continued preparations for war. To promote unification, Mandela kept the existing presidential staff and appointed the broadest possible coalition in his cabinet. He made it his priority to create "the Rainbow Nation."

The national sport of white South Africa was rugby, and their beloved team was the Springboks. Most blacks hated the Springboks because they were a symbol of segregation and white domination. But Mandela masterly strategized to use the Springboks to achieve national unity. And in Johannesburg, in 1995, the Springboks beat Australia in overtime to win the World Cup. It was a galvanizing national moment, masterfully portrayed in John Carlin's book, *Playing the Enemy,*[10] and in the 2009 movie, *Invictus.* After the game, Mandela shook hands with the Springbok captain and thanked him for what he had done for the country. With spectators weeping, the reply was, "No, Mr. President. Thank *you* for what *you* have done for our country."

AFTER THE PRESIDENCY

Mandela was in office five years from 1994 to 1999 and then declined to run for a second term. Prison life and public life had been hard on family life. His marriage as a young man lasted 13 years and brought four children. A daughter died at age nine months, and a son was killed in a car crash at age twenty-five while Mandela was in prison. Before imprisonment, he married Winnie and they had two daughters; shortly after his prison release they divorced. Mandela remarried on his 80th birthday.

Nelson Mandela has received more than 250 awards including the 1993 Nobel Peace Prize and the U.S. Presidential Medal of Freedom. As this book was in the final stage of publication, December, 2013, my daughter called me with the news that, at age 95, Nelson Mandela was dead. I feel a loss – almost as losing a father. I feel gratitude that this mega-man has been in my life – and will continue to be. The parting words of his autobiography seem applicable – he is taking his moment to rest. And perhaps his long walk is indeed not ended because of those who continue walking that long road to freedom.

> I have walked that long road to freedom. I have tried not to falter; I have made missteps along the way. But I have discovered the secret that after climbing a great hill, one only finds that there are many more hills to climb. I have taken a moment here to rest, to steal a view of the glorious vista that surrounds me, to look back on the distance I have come. But I can rest only for

a moment, for with freedom comes responsibilities, and I dare not linger, for my long walk is not yet ended.[11]

QUESTIONS TO PONDER AND DISCUSS:

1. Can *you* participate in a do-it-yourself "University"?

2. In your opinion, what was central in making Nelson Mandela a great man?

3. When *you* achieve "freedom," what is *your* mission?

A QUESTION FOR A WRITTEN ANSWER:

What is the one lesson for you to remember from Nelson Mandela?

Afflicted with deprivation, torture, and humiliation — but Unbroken!

3

Louis Zamperini
1917 –

Louie Zamperini is a story of opposites. He went from hoodlum to setting a world interscholastic record for the mile run. He went from a superb physical specimen to a 67-pound skeleton. He went from Olympic hero to being listed as killed in action. He went from hate to forgiveness. He went from an unbelieving drunk to a Christian preacher. He had it all.

Louie was born in 1917, the son of Italian immigrants and was raised in Torrance, southern California. Of the early days he said, "I was just a social misfit, the proverbial square peg who couldn't fit into the round hole like the rest." He had a talent for trouble – fighting, stealing, gang activity and more.

Louie also had a talent for running, which turned his life around. In high school, he set a world interscholastic record and was awarded a scholarship to the University of Southern California. He set a national collegiate mile record which he held for fifteen years. At age 19, he went to the 1936 Berlin Olympics and finished eighth in the 5,000 meter run (after gaining 12 pounds eating the ship's food on the way over). He was determined to enter the next Olympics and win. The opportunity never came.

Instead, it was World War II that came and the 1940 Olympics were cancelled. At age 24, Louie enlisted in the United States Army Air Force, was commissioned a second lieutenant, and became a bombardier on a B-24 bomber. Louie's plane crashed in the middle of the Pacific Ocean killing eight of the eleven crew members. One man later died and Louie and a companion were on the raft 45 days and drifted 2,000 miles. They only had a small amount of water and a few candy bars. They subsisted on captured rainwater, small fish, and birds. Louie went from 155 pounds to approximately 67. They held off shark attacks and were nearly capsized in a storm. They were strafed by a Japanese bomber who put 48 bullet holes in their raft.

The experience of living forty-five days under desperate conditions provided time and motivation for thought. Louie found that, away from the noise of civilization, the silence offered his mind freedom. His mind could roam anywhere and he found it was quick and clear and his imagination was limitless. Without interruption, he was in awe of his power of concentration. "I tried to remember my life as far back as I could . . . . To my surprise it brought up events I didn't even realize I'd forgotten."

Louie's story is told in his autobiography *Devil at My Heels*,[1] and his biography *Unbroken, A World War II Story of Survival, Resilience, and Redemption*.[2] *Unbroken, by* Laura Hillenbrand, became a #1 New York Times bestseller and is being made into a movie.

Following are a few of Louie's comments from *Devil at My Heels*.

But rather than give in, I made myself a promise: no matter what lay ahead, I'd never think about dying, only about living.[3]

Through it all I never lost my sense that life could be beautiful. I kept my zest for living, morning and night. I'd made it this far and refused to give up because all my life I had always finished the race.[4]

But because we'd survived the crash I had to at least consider the possibility of some kind of divine intervention. Just to be on the safe side, I thanked God for saving our lives. My buddies prayed with me. Of course, on life rafts that's what you mostly do: you pray.[5] [He offered a prayer that would later come back to haunt him]. Answer my prayers now, and I promise if I get home through all this and whatever is to come, I'll serve You for the rest of my life.[6]

They reached an atoll in the Marshall Islands and fell into the hands of Japanese captors. After beatings and torture, Louie was taken to Japan. Back home, he was listed as missing in action. After a year, he was listed as killed in action.

In Japan, atrocities escalated. The most brutal of the guards was nicknamed "the Bird," who took a personal disliking to Louie and singled him out for regular and unmerciful humiliation and beatings. The torture of the prisoners included clubbing, jamming penknives under fingernails, or tearing off fingernails. Then there was the "water cure" – tipping a prisoner backward, holding his mouth shut, and pouring water up his nose until he passed out. The men had to do pushups over the latrine troughs until they collapsed facedown. Louie was assigned the job of cleaning out the pig pen with no tools, only his hands. He ate the pig's food to help protect him from beriberi.

Louie described conditions in the prison camp.

At night huge rats would run over those of us sleeping up high. If you made any attempt to knock them away, they were certain to attack with a vengeance – and no one wanted to be bitten by these filthy aggressive creatures.

Although we all had shoes, most of us walked the two miles to work barefoot in the March snow and ice, our feet wrapped in rags, because the Bird had a rule:

whoever had dirty shoes got beaten and had to lick them clean. The latrines were overflowing and the men had diarrhea. When they got back, the Bird ordered them 'you lick bottom of boots or die.'

Every day, three times a day, we were served an awful red grain…along with dried ferns and seaweed. The grain tasted bitter and foul. Often it contained pebbles and bits of wire that chipped my teeth and left my mouth bleeding and raw.[7]

The food was infested with rat droppings and maggots. The men were ravenous and pulled up weeds and ate them. Their only drinking water was from a reservoir containing water from rice paddies fertilized with human excrement. Ninety percent of the men were afflicted with dysentery. Most of them had beriberi and some went blind from malnutrition.

After prisoners endured affliction more than two years, the war ended. Altogether, 34,648 Americans had been held prisoner by Japan; more than 37 percent of them died from mistreatment.[8]

Louis Zamperini, already known in America for past athletic achievements, now came home from the war a hero. He gave speeches and made radio appearances. In 1946 he fell in love and married. From all appearance, it seemed he was living the dream.

But, all was not well. One of the chapter titles in his autobiography is, "The Empty Hero." Louie tried to get back into running but it didn't work. He had nightmares about the Bird and he suffered severe anxiety. He regularly awoke screaming and soaked in sweat. He was afraid to sleep. There was still the torture and the horror. He began to drink heavily and was consumed in self-pity and depression. He made a resolve – he was going to kill the Bird, and the hatred in that thought consumed him.[9]

[Cynthia was] determined to get a divorce. Our situation, she insisted, was hopeless. I didn't have a steady income. I'd been 'taken' by different people. I drank. I was angry. Unstable. She loved me, but that was no longer enough . . . . I'd failed her. I'd failed my family. I'd failed myself.[10]

Louie had kept Cynthia from going to church for two years. Then one day she commanded Louie to drop her off at the church. Louie seethed, "I couldn't explain my hatred of religion, of God." Her neighbors encouraged Cynthia to attend a tent meeting for the Billy Graham Crusade, and she recommitted her life to God. After a week of arguing with Louie, he agreed to go to the tent meeting. Halfway through, he grabbed Cynthia by the arm and they left. But something had stirred in Louie. Somehow, Cynthia got him to go back. This time he lasted a little longer before he pulled Cynthia into the aisle to leave. But, he paused as he remembered his vow on the raft, "I promise if I get home through all this . . . I'll serve You for the rest of my life."

After the hesitation in the aisle, instead of turning left to the exit, he turned right to the stand. There was conferencing with a counselor, there was contemplation, there was prayer, there was asking Jesus to come into his life, there was a commitment to keep his vow on the raft. Following is Louie's description.

I waited. And then, true to His promise, He came into my heart and my life. The moment was more than remarkable; it was the most *realistic* experience I'd ever had.

I found Cynthia waiting in the audience, and she threw her arms around me. I looked at her and knew in my heart, as if it had always been so, that I was through drinking, through smoking, through with everything. My lifelong desire for revenge had disappeared, including my need to get even with the Japanese and the Bird. . . . 'I'm through with my past life,' I told Cynthia.

'I'm through.' She smiled, lit with the light of the miracle she knew had occurred.

I had a lot of liquor at home . . . I poured it all down the drain . . . I threw my cigarettes in the trash. . . . When she saw me emptying the bottles into the sink, she was on cloud nine. She knew I'd undergone a real conversion. 'Now I'm not going to get a divorce,' she said.

The next morning I woke up and realized I hadn't had a nightmare about the Bird. And to this day I've never had another. . . . I believed hating was the same as getting even. . . . All I did was destroy myself with my hate[11]

Louie was asked to tell his story to groups and became a sought-after Christian speaker. He returned to Japan to meet with his old prison guards who were now in prison themselves as war criminals. Upon meeting them, he stepped toward them and with a radiant smile, to the amazement of all, he extended his hand or a hug to those who had inflicted such degradation. He told them he had forgiven them. But, one was missing – the Bird. He was told the Bird had stabbed himself to death. Louie was amazed that what he now felt for this man who had so horrendously abused him, was only compassion.

For his 81st birthday in 1998, Louie returned to Japan to run a leg in the Olympic Torch relay for the Winter Olympics. There he received startling news – the Bird was alive and had embarked on a career in insurance. Louie attempted to arrange a meeting. The Bird declined. Louie wrote him a letter.

As a result of my prisoner of war experience under your unwarranted and unreasonable punishment, my post-war life became a nightmare. It was not so much due to the pain and suffering as it was the tension of stress and humiliation that caused me to hate with a vengeance.

The post-war nightmares caused my life to crumble, but thanks to a confrontation with God . . . love replaced the hate I had for you.

I returned to Japan in 1952 and was graciously allowed to address all the Japanese war criminals at Sugamo Prison. . . . Like the others, I also forgave you.

- Louis Zamperini.[12]

Louis Zamperini spoke throughout the United States and several foreign countries telling his story and particularly focusing on his religious faith. His old high school's athletic stadium is called Zamperini Stadium. The entrance plaza at USC's track & field stadium was named Louis Zamperini Plaza. His home town renamed its airport Zamperini Field. At this writing in 2013, Louis Zamperini is still living actively at the age of 96. He has taken up scuba diving, skiing, glacier climbing, flying and skateboarding. He told a friend that the last time he could remember being angry was more than forty years before.

QUESTIONS TO PONDER AND DISCUSS:

1. What can be a lesson regarding the deprivation and atrocities inflicted on Louie Zamperini?

2. What is your reaction to Louie's personal transformation?

3. What is your reaction to Louie's forgiveness of his guards and "the Bird"?

A QUESTION FOR A WRITTEN ANSWER:

What is the one lesson for you to remember from Louis Zamperini?

"Bless you, prison, for having been in my life!"

4
Alexandr Solzhenitsyn
1918 - 2008

"Bless you, prison, for having been in my life;" such a bizarre statement! It becomes even more startling knowing that Alexandr Solzhenitsyn's promising military career was abruptly ended when he was sentenced to eight years in a brutal Soviet prison camp system. Only one in six prisoners survived. Alexandr survived to become a reformer and a writer. He was awarded the Nobel Prize in literature.

Alexandr Solzhenitsyn was born in Russia in 1918. His father was killed before his birth, and he was raised by his widowed mother and aunt in lowly circumstances. He achieved a university degree, obtained the rank of captain in the Soviet army, and was twice-decorated. However, in a private letter he criticized Stalin's handling of the war. As a result, without notice he was arrested, stripped of his uniform, and convicted of anti-Soviet propaganda. He spent eight years paying for his crime. At the end of his prison term in 1953, Solzhenitsyn was sent into exile.

There are many possible reactions to such mistreatment. Solzhenitsyn's response was to write. He wrote of his prison experience and published a book which gained acclaim, *One Day in the Life of*

Ivan Denisovich.[1] It is the story of a poor and uneducated peasant in a Soviet labor camp. The living conditions were almost intolerable. Ivan slept in his clothes on a rotten, thin mattress. Food was meager and poor. Clothing was deficient in the Siberian cold. Guards forced prisoners to undress for body searches at temperatures of forty degrees below zero. There is much in the book that is autobiographical of Solzhenitsyn.

> This was the toughest moment – when you lined up for roll call in the morning. Into the bitter cold in the darkness with an empty belly.[2]

> It was the beginning of a new year . . . and [Ivan] was allowed to write two letters home this year. He'd sent his last one off in July and had an answer in October.[3]

> Rejoice that you are in prison. Here you can think of your soul [Said by Alyoshka, a fellow-prisoner].[4]

At this point, Solzhenitsyn's writing was only a warm-up. He abhorred the Soviet prison-camp system and he wrote another book documenting its atrocities. That book became one of the most consequential books of the 20th century. He wrote about the surprise arrests to remove possible dissidents and fill labor camps. He exposed the horrendous interrogation techniques that were applied until guilt was admitted. He described the unlivable conditions and the cattle-car transports in the dead of winter. He told of a railroad camp during the winter of 1941-1942; the prisoner population dwindled from 50,000 to 10,000 – 40,000 deaths through deprivation. A canal was built at the expense of a quarter million corpses.

Citizens could be arrested for anything under Article 58. A deaf and dumb carpenter, laying floors with no nail or hook for his jacket and cap, hung them on a bust of Lenin. He was arrested for counter-revolutionary agitation and sentenced to 10 years imprisonment. A child was sentenced to eight years imprisonment for having a pocketful of potatoes. Once in camp, prisoners could be sentenced to second and third terms for no reason. There were punishment cells where prisoners were stripped down to their underwear and given little food, even when the temperatures fell to 58 degrees below zero. Children were separated from their parents and became beasts in a survival of the fittest.

The book was *Gulag Archipelago*.[5] It sold thirty million copies in thirty-five languages and earned Solzhenitsyn the Nobel Prize in Literature. The book includes a section titled, "The Soul and Barbed Wire," providing a glimpse into his prison soul.

ACCEPTANCE OF MISSION

"I came to understand that it was my duty to take upon my shoulders a share of their [fellow prisoners'] common burden – and to bear it to the last man, until it crushed us."[6]

THE SPARK OF GOD

"After all, once upon a time a weak little spark of God was breathed into [prisoners] too – is it not true? So what has become of it now?"[7]

PERSONAL CHANGE

It was on rotting prison straw that I felt the first stirrings of good in myself.

Imprisonment begins to transform your former character in an astonishing way. To transform it in a direction most unexpected to you. . . . Once upon a time you were sharply intolerant. You were constantly in a rush. And you were constantly short of time. And now you have time with interest. You are surfeited with it, with its months and its years, behind you and ahead of you – and a beneficial calming fluid pours through your blood vessels – patience. You are ascending.[8]

Here is a rewarding and inexhaustible direction for your thoughts: Reconsider all your previous life. Remember everything you did that was bad and shameful and take thought – can't you possibly correct it now?[9]

But the day when I deliberately let myself sink to the bottom and felt it firm under my feet – the hard, rock bottom which is the same for all – was the beginning of the most important years in my life, the years which put the finishing touches to my character. From then onward there seem to have been no upheavals in my life, and I have been faithful to the views and habits acquired at that time.[10]

The meaning of earthly existence lies not, as we have grown used to thinking, in prospering, but . . . in the development of the soul.[11]

INTERNAL FREEDOM

[It is not] possible to liberate anyone who has not first become liberated in his own soul.[12] . . . It is a good thing to think in prison . . . and this is the main thing, there are no meetings. For ten years you are free from all kinds of meetings! Is that not mountain air? The camp keepers do not encroach at all on your thoughts. . . . And this results in a sensation of freedom of much greater magnitude than the freedom of one's feet. . . . A free head – now is that not an advantage of life in the Archipelago? And there is one more freedom: No one can deprive you of your family and property – you have already been deprived of them. What does not exist – not even God can take away. And this is a basic freedom.[13]

ASSOCIATES, FRIENDSHIP

Formerly you never forgave anyone. You judged people without mercy. And you praised people with equal lack of moderation. And now an understanding mildness has become the basis of your uncategorical judgments. You have come to realize your own weakness – and you can therefore understand the weakness of others. And be astonished at another's strength.[14]

I was startled not for the first time or the last to realize what far from ordinary souls are concealed within deceptively ordinary exteriors.[15]

And how many of us come to realize: It is particularly in slavery that for the first time we have learned to recognize genuine friendship![16]

After Solzhenitsyn's release, letters were exchanged with fellow prisoners for many years. "In our day, if you get a letter completely free from self-pity, genuinely optimistic – it can only be from a former [prisoner]. They are used to the worst the world can do, and nothing can depress them."[17]

THE CAPACITY OF MEMORY

Memory was the only hidey-hole in which you could keep what you had written and carry it through all the searches and journeys under escort. In the early days I had little confidence in the powers of memory, [yet] no longer burdened with frivolous and superfluous knowledge, a prisoner's memory is astonishingly capacious, and can expand indefinitely. We have too little faith in memory![18]

Solzhenitsyn used something like rosary beads as a system to help him remember his thoughts. He estimated, by the end of his sentence, he had written and memorized 12,000 lines.[19]

SUMMARY

Ponder Solzhenitsyn's prison summary. "I turn back to the years of my imprisonment and say, sometimes to the astonishment of those about me: 'Bless you, prison!' . . . I nourished my soul there, and I say without hesitation: 'Bless you, prison, for having been in my life!'"[20]

CONCLUSION

Many more adventures lay ahead for Alexandr Solzhenitsyn. For agitating against the system, in 1974 Solzhenitsyn was arrested, stripped of his Soviet citizenship, and deported to Germany. He moved to Switzerland and then to the United States. He was awarded an honorary Literary Degree from Harvard University. While admiring local democracy in America, he was critical of the materialism in modern western culture and criticized the spiritual vacuum he saw. "The human soul longs for things higher, warmer, and purer than those offered by today's mass living habits . . . by TV stupor and by intolerable music."

In 1990, Solzhenitsyn's Soviet citizenship was restored and four years later, after 18 years, he returned to Russia with his wife who had become a United States citizen. Their sons stayed behind in the United States and became U.S. citizens. Alexandr Solzhenitsyn died of heart failure near Moscow in 2008 at the age of 89.

QUESTIONS TO PONDER AND DISCUSS:

1. What does Solzhenitsyn mean: "[It is not] possible to liberate anyone who has not first become liberated in his own soul."?

2. Select one quotation from Solzhenitsyn that is meaningful to you. Why?

3. Explain what Solzhenitsyn meant when he said, "Bless you, prison, for having been in my life."

A QUESTION FOR A WRITTEN ANSWER:

What is the one lesson for you to remember from Alexandr Solzhenitsyn?

"To forgive is to set a prisoner free and discover that the prisoner was you."

5

Corrie ten Boom
1892 – 1983

What do you do when SS troops are rounding up Jews for death and you might be able to save some of them at the peril of your own life? What do you do with an informer who has caused your arrest and the death of your father and sister? What do you do with a Nazi guard who wants to shake your hand? Corrie ten Boom had to decide.

Corrie ten Boom was a Dutch Jew at the time the Nazis invaded the Netherlands in 1940. In her fifties, Corrie had no family of her own and lived with her parents. The Nazis began rounding up Jews for the death camps. Corrie and her family decided to provide a hiding place for Jews whose lives were in danger. At the end of February, 1944, a fellow Dutch citizen notified the Nazis of the ten Boom's activities. Corrie, her father, and sister Betsie (seven years older) were arrested, separated, and incarcerated in Scheveningen prison. Months later, Corrie learned her elderly father died nine days after his imprisonment.

Corrie ten Boom's inspirational journey of survival and forgiveness is told in her books *The Hiding Place*[1] and *Prison Letters*.[2] Corrie was assigned to solitary confinement for several months, which induced severe loneliness. "I was as starved for the sight of a human face as for the food." When she was able to take a shower, "Even in the strict silence this human closeness was joy and strength . . . I thought, they are all my sisters. How rich is anyone who can simply see human faces!"

Any relationship was welcomed.

> I was not alone much longer: into my solitary cell came a small busy black ant. . . . I crouched down and admired the marvelous design of legs and body. After a while, he disappeared through a crack in the floor. But when my evening piece of bread appeared on the door shelf, I scattered some crumbs and to my joy he popped out almost at once. He picked up a heroic piece, struggled down the hole with it and came back for more. It was the beginning of a relationship.[4]

A letter to her sister signaled Corrie had changed her feelings about solitary confinement as she took advantage of the introspection it provided.

> I have miraculously adjusted to this lonely life, but I am in communion with God. . . . I am grateful that I am alone, me who loves company and people so much! I see my sins more clearly, my own SELF in capitals, and much more superficiality in me. . . . The Lord is close to me as never before in my life. . . . My soul is very peaceful. Fortunately, I have overcome the shock of the last months.[5]

Corrie was transferred to Vught prison and was overjoyed to be together with her sister Betsie. Betsie was the exemplar of compassion. Looking at the guards, Betsie exclaimed, "Corrie, if people can be taught to hate, they can be taught to love! We must find the way, you and I, no matter how long it takes."

> I glanced at the matron seated at the desk ahead of us.
> I saw a gray uniform and a visored hat; Betsie saw a

wounded human being. And I wondered, not for the first time, what sort of a person she was, this sister of mine . . . what kind of road she followed while I trudged beside her on the all-too-solid earth.[6]

Corrie and Betsie discovered the identity of the Dutchman who had betrayed them. A man named Jan Vogel had caused their arrest and the death of their father.

And I knew that if Jan Vogel stood in front of me now I could kill him. . . . All of me ached with the violence of my feelings . . . . What puzzled me all this time was Betsie. She had suffered everything I had and yet she seemed to carry no burden of rage.

'Betsie!' I hissed one dark night . . . 'don't you feel anything about Jan Vogel? Doesn't it bother you?' And again, it was Betsie who rose above the ordinary and merged with divinity.

'Oh yes, Corrie! Terribly! I've felt for him ever since I knew – and pray for him whenever his name comes into my mind. How dreadfully he must be suffering!'

For a long time I lay silent in the huge shadowy barracks restless with the sighs, snores, and stirrings of hundreds of women. Once again I had the feeling that this sister with whom I had spent all my life belonged somehow to another order of beings. Wasn't she telling me in her gentle way that I was as guilty as Jan Vogel? . . . 'Lord Jesus,' I whispered into the lumpy ticking of the bed, 'I forgive Jan Vogel as I pray that You will forgive me. I have done him great damage. Bless him now, and his family . . . .' That night for the first time since our betrayer had a name I slept deep and dreamlessly until the whistle summoned us to roll call.[7]

The killing that went on around them was terrifying. "Then rifle fire split the air. Around us women began to weep. A second volley. A third. For two hours the executions went on. Someone counted. More than seven hundred male prisoners were killed that day."

Corrie and Betsie were transferred to Ravensbruck in Germany, a notorious extermination camp for women. All possessions were taken away including clothes on their backs. Somehow, they were able to keep hidden a small copy of parts of the New Testament. And they reveled in its infinite message of hope.

> From morning until lights-out, whenever we were not in ranks for roll call, our Bible was the center of an ever-widening circle of help and hope. Like waifs clustered around a blazing fire, we gathered about it, holding out our hearts to its warmth and light. The blacker the night around us grew, the brighter and truer and more beautiful burned the word of God. . . . Sometimes I would slip the Bible from its little sack with hands that shook, so mysterious had it become to me. It was new; it had just been written. I marveled sometimes that the ink was dry.[8]

Outside prison walls, religious denominations and creeds focus on *differences*. They erect divisions, separateness, and often animosity. But, prison circumstances can set aside external differences and enhance commonality.

> They were services like no others, these times in Barracks 28. A single meeting might include a recital of the Magnificat in Latin by a group of Roman Catholics, a whispered hymn by some Lutherans, and a sotto-voce chant by Eastern Orthodox women. With each moment the crowd around us would swell, packing the nearby platforms, hanging over the edges, until the high structures groaned and swayed.[9]

Betsie even thanked God for fleas. This was because the affliction kept the guards out of the prisoner's quarters so they could keep their forbidden Bible and hold study groups. Betsie's mysterious influence was that of a saint.

> What a difference since Betsie had come to this room! Where before this had been the moment for scuffles and cursing, tonight the huge dormitory buzzed with 'Sorry!' 'Excuse me!' And 'No harm done!' Side by side, in the sanctuary of God's fleas, Betsie and I ministered the word of God to all in the room. We sat by deathbeds that became doorways of heaven. We watched women who had lost everything grow rich in hope.[10]

But Betsie was gravely ill. Corrie leaned down to the stretcher on the floor to make out her sister's last words. "[We] must tell people what we have learned here. We must tell them that there is no pit so deep that He is not deeper still. They will listen to us, Corrie, because we have been here."[11]

Within days of Betsie's death, Corrie was released from prison. She wrote, "It was not until December 28, 1944, when through a miracle, I was set free, just one week before all women my age and older were put to death."

Corrie returned to the Netherlands with a mission. She opened a rehabilitation center in what had been a concentration camp. Though she had been betrayed, she sheltered the jobless Dutch who previously collaborated with Germans during the occupation. She traveled the world as a public speaker, appeared in more than sixty countries, and wrote several books. She was intent on sharing the true meaning of Christianity and the message framed on her wall at home, "Whatever in our life is hardest to bear, love can transform into beauty."

She wrote a letter to Jan Vogel, the man who had betrayed her family. It included the following words.

I went through 10 months of concentration camp. My father died after 9 days of imprisonment. My sister died in prison, too. The harm you planned was turned into good for me by God. I came nearer to Him . . . I have forgiven you everything.[12]

At age 85 years of age, Corrie ten Boom moved to Placentia California. Her first stroke rendered her unable to speak. The second stroke resulted in paralysis. For five years, she lived as an invalid until the third stroke took her life on her 91st birthday, April 15, 1983.

There is a final, captivating story at the end of *The Hiding Place*.

It was at a church service in Munich that I saw him, the former S.S. man who had stood guard at the shower room door in the processing center at Ravensbruck. He was the first of our actual jailers that I had seen since that time. And suddenly it was all there – the roomful of mocking men, the heaps of clothing.

He came up to me as the church was emptying, beaming and bowing. 'How grateful I am for your message, *Fraulein*.' He said, 'To think that, as you say, He has washed my sins away!'

His hand was thrust out to shake mine. And I, who had preached so often to the people in Bloemendaal the need to forgive, kept my hand at my side.

Even as the angry, vengeful thoughts boiled through me, I saw the sin of them. Jesus Christ had died for this man; was I going to ask for more? Lord Jesus, I prayed, forgive me and help me to forgive him.

I tried to smile, I struggled to raise my hand. I could not. I felt nothing, not the slightest spark of warmth or charity. And so again I breathed a silent prayer. Jesus, I cannot forgive him. Give me Your forgiveness.

As I took his hand the most incredible thing happened. From my shoulder along my arm and through my hand a current seemed to pass from me to him, while into my heart sprang a love for this stranger that almost overwhelmed me.[13]

Another resident of the Netherlands, Lewis B. Smedes, wrote a book on forgiveness. Following is one of his statements describing Corrie's lesson, "To forgive is to set a prisoner free and discover that the prisoner was you."[14]

QUESTIONS TO PONDER AND DISCUSS:

1. What was it about Betsie that allowed her to have a positive influence?

2. Is forgiveness really the key to escaping one's own personal imprisonment? Explain.

3. Have you forgiven?

A QUESTION FOR A WRITTEN ANSWER:

What is the one lesson for you to remember from Corrie and Betsie ten Boom?

"He who has a *Why* to live for can bear almost any *How*."

6

Viktor E. Frankl
1905 - 1997

Viktor Frankl was a Jewish psychiatrist who survived four Nazi concentration camps where the odds of survival were no more than 1 to 28. Being a psychiatrist gave him a penetrating view of suffering and survival. The primary survival weapon he discovered was *meaning*. A favorite summarizing statement of Frankl came from Friedrich Nietzsche, "He who has a *why* to live for can bear almost any *how*."

Viktor Frankl was born in Vienna in 1905. He filled requirements to become a doctor and psychiatrist at the University of Vienna. In 1942, he and his wife and parents were deported to a Nazi Jewish ghetto. From there, he was transferred to Auschwitz. His wife, mother, father, and brother died at Auschwitz. Frankl was liberated in 1945 by the Americans.

Frankl documented his time in concentration camps in his book, *Man's Search for Meaning*.[1] The book has been translated into 24 languages and sold more than 10 million copies. The Library of Congress called the book one of the ten most influential books of the twentieth century.

Let's begin with a brief snapshot of conditions in the concentration camps.

> We had to wear the same shirts for half a year, until they had lost all appearance of being shirts.

> [We lived on] 10-1/2 ounces of bread (often less) and 1-3/4 pints of thin soup per day.

> When the last layers of subcutaneous fat had vanished, and we looked like skeletons disguised with skin and rags, we could watch our bodies beginning to devour themselves. The organism digested its own protein, and the muscles disappeared.

> One morning I heard someone, whom I knew to be brave and dignified, cry like a child because he finally had to go to the snowy marching grounds in his bare feet, as his shoes were too shrunken for him to wear.[2]

Viktor Frankl became prisoner number 119,104. He adopted the philosophy of Friedrich Nietzsche, "That which does not kill me, makes me stronger."[3]

At times, survival was unpredictable. For instance, at Auschwitz it was the "finger game." As prisoners filed by, if the finger of the SS man pointed right, the prisoner went to the work camps. If it pointed to the left, as it did most of the time, it meant the crematorium. And of those who went to the work camps, most did not survive the hardships. Yet, though the conditions were abhorrent, there were survivors.

What are the critical questions? When only one of twenty-eight survived, what was a key element in survival? Further, of those who survived the hell of the work camps, a few became saints. How? I have chosen an interview format to ask Dr. Frankl questions; his answers are from his book.

MEANING

Dr. Frankl, it seems curious that your book about survival is titled *Man's Search for Meaning* – with the emphasis on "Meaning." The therapy you developed and promote you call Logotherapy; "logos" is a Greek word which means "meaning." You have said, "There is nothing in the world, I venture to say, that would so effectively help one to survive even the worst conditions as the knowledge that there is a *meaning* in one's life." How did you come to that conclusion?

In a last violent protest against the hopelessness of imminent death, I sensed my spirit piercing through the enveloping gloom. I felt it transcend that hopeless, meaningless world, and from some where I heard a victorious 'Yes' in answer to my question of the existence of an ultimate purpose.[4]

[At Auschwitz] Those who knew that there was a task waiting for them to fulfill were most apt to survive.[5]

What about today? Unlike Auschwitz, we typically have most of our basic needs met. Do you still find meaninglessness today?

So many patients complain today [of] the feeling of the total and ultimate meaninglessness of their lives. They lack the awareness of a meaning worth living for. They are haunted by the experience of their inner emptiness, a void within themselves; they are caught in that situation which I have called the 'existential vacuum' . . . loss of the feeling that life is meaningful.[6]

IS THERE REALLY A CHOICE?

You said beatings occurred on the slightest provocation, sometimes for no reason at all. You further reported that, "Fifteen hundred captives were cooped up in a shed built to accommodate probably two hundred at the most . . . Nine men [slept] directly on the boards. Two blankets were shared by each nine men." Under these conditions, were people really able to make choices? What could they choose?

We can answer these questions from experience as well as on principle. The experiences of camp life show that man does have a choice of action. There were enough examples, often of a heroic nature, which proved that apathy could be overcome, irritability suppressed. Man *can* preserve a vestige of spiritual freedom, of independence of mind, even in such terrible conditions of psychic and physical stress.[7]

In the final analysis it becomes clear that the sort of person the prisoner became was the result of an inner decision, and not the result of camp influences alone. Fundamentally, therefore, any man can, even under such circumstances, decide what shall become of him – mentally and spiritually.[8]

You mention heroic examples. What do those examples look like in a concentration camp?

We who lived in concentration camps can remember the men who walked through the huts comforting others, giving away their last piece of bread. They may have been few in number, but they offer sufficient proof that everything can be taken from a man but one thing: the last of the human freedoms – to choose one's attitude in any given set of circumstances, to choose one's own way.[9]

THE PLACE OF LOVE

Most of the time your feet were wet and cold; frostbite and chilblains made every step torture. Your father, your mother, your brother, and your wife died in concentration camps. You didn't even know if your wife was alive or dead. Yet, you never spoke of hate. Instead, you adopted love as part of your inner life. This seems astonishing!

> *The salvation of man is through love and in love.* I understood how a man who has nothing left in this world still may know bliss, be it only for a brief moment, in the contemplation of his beloved. In a position of utter desolation, when man cannot express himself in positive action, when his only achievement may consist in enduring his sufferings in the right way – an honorable way – in such a position man can, through loving contemplation of the image he carries of his beloved, achieve fulfillment.[10]

SPIRITUALITY IN THE CAMPS

In such desolate conditions as a concentration camp, one might expect spirituality to dwindle. It seems many would curse God and die. Yet you indicated this was not typically the case. You speak of an inner spiritual life – what does that mean?

> In spite of all the enforced physical and mental primitiveness of the life in a concentration camp, it was possible for spiritual life to deepen. Sensitive people who were used to a rich intellectual life . . . were able to retreat from their terrible surroundings to a life of inner riches and spiritual freedom. Only in this way can one explain the apparent paradox that some prisoners of a less hardy make-up often seemed to survive camp life better than did those of a robust nature.[11]

> The religious interest of the prisoners, as far and as soon as it developed, was the most sincere imaginable. . . . Most impressive in this connection were improvised prayers or services in the corner of a hut, or in the darkness of the locked cattle truck.[12]

When you could, you tried to teach your fellow-prisoners. What did you tell them?

> What was really needed was a fundamental change in our attitude toward life. We had to learn ourselves and furthermore, we had to teach the despairing men, that *it did not really matter what we expected from life, but rather what life expected from us.*[13]
>
> Every human being has the freedom to change at any instant . . . a human being is a self-transcending being.[14]

In the concentration camp, finally the white flag was raised and Viktor Frankl and the other survivors were free. Yet, the occasion was not what one might expect.

> It would be quite wrong to think that we went mad with joy. . . . We had literally lost the ability to feel pleased and had to relearn it slowly . . . . [The body] began to eat ravenously, for hours and days, even half the night. It is amazing what quantities one can eat.
>
> I walked through the country past flowered meadows, for miles and miles…there was nothing but the wide earth and sky and the larks' jubilation and the freedom of space. I stopped, looked around, and up to the sky – and then I went down on my knees.[15]

Since that time, Dr. Frankl has taught seminars all over the world, received 29 honorary doctoral degrees, and published 39 books (translated into 40 languages). He remarried at age 42, became an avid mountain climber, and earned his pilot's license at age 67. He died in 1997 at age 92.

QUESTIONS TO PONDER AND DISCUSS:

1. A central message of Viktor Frankl is that we can choose our attitude under any circumstance. What is one attitude you could change that would add quality to your life?

2. Under the worst deprivation imaginable, there were still "heroic" examples of prisoners who gave their last piece of bread and extended comfort. How were they able to do that?

3. The following is a central message of Viktor Frankl, "He who has a *why* to live for can bear almost any *how*." What is *your* "*why*"?

A QUESTION FOR A WRITTEN ANSWER:

What is the one lesson for you to remember from Viktor Frankl?

The University of San Quentin

7
Bill Dallas
1960 –

Bill Dallas graduated with honors from Vanderbilt University. While he excelled in academics, he missed a course in ethics which put him on the fast track to calamity. He was recycled to another university – the University of San Quentin where he graduated magna cum laude.

Of his early years Bill Dallas stated, "My upbringing had been neither normal nor especially healthy." His mother was bipolar, fought alcoholism, and was sexually molested by her father. In an interview he acknowledged, "I had so little self-esteem. Didn't get affirmation from my family. Didn't really get affirmation from anybody."

He achieved dazzling success in the San Francisco bay area real estate market. But, there was a flip side. "Women were my life, a lot of drinking, a lot of drugs; anything to keep me numbed up until I went to bed at night; because I didn't want to slow down to have to think about what was going on inside of me. And so I just wanted to keep a very fast-paced life." Speaking of fast, he owned a BMW and a Porsche and, oh yes, he did modeling. By the time he was 30, he was Bill Dallas – wonder boy.

But he didn't take into account his illegitimate business practices or the real estate crash of the early 1990s. His real estate empire crumbled. He was convicted of grand theft and embezzlement and sentenced to five years in prison. At age 31, he went from "king of the party animals" to number H64741 at San Quentin. He wrote a book called, *Lessons from San Quentin, Everything I Needed to Know about Life I Learned in Prison.*[1]

Let's skip ahead. After Bill Dallas was released from San Quentin, he slept on the floor of his parents' one-bedroom apartment, and wherever he went he rode the bus. He ended up getting a sales job with a video production company.

Bill Dallas had previously fathered a son who was eight years of age when he went to prison. He hadn't had much of a relationship with him, but after prison, he decided the relationship with his son was a priority. After his release, he made a declaration to his boy.

> 'Son, I want you to know that I am in your life forever. Even if someone offered me a billion dollars to move across the country, I wouldn't even *think* about taking it. I will never leave you.' . . . After that, our relationship reached a whole new level. . . . God also blessed me with a wonderful wife, Bettina . . . and I have a wonderful daughter, Amanda, and we live in a comfortable home on the coast of northern California.[2]

Along the way, Bill Dallas became president and CEO of Church Communication Network. CCN is a satellite and Internet communications company delivering video training seminars and conferences to more than 6,000 churches across North America.

Following are the questions I would ask Bill Dallas if I had the opportunity of meeting him. His responses are quotations from his book.

TRANSITION.

Mr. Dallas, you sound highly optimistic, but it didn't start out that way in San Quentin.

> One day I found myself curled up in the fetal position on the prison yard ground, moaning and sobbing. My deepest desire was simply to die. Life had gotten the best of me, and I was ready to roll over and give up. I had no apparent reason to continue now that justice had crushed me and my life was irreparably ruined. I spent an entire month – a month – curled into that ball in the prison yard. Inmates passing by looked at me with disgust. I was not a man; I was just a pathetic, miserable, self-absorbed sack of flesh and bones.[3]

A fellow-inmate told him to get up, took him to the prison television station and talked the manager into giving him a job sweeping the floor. That began the transformation. He ended up learning everything he could about television production – running cameras, designing sets, directing programs, producing special events, being an on-air talent.

Bill summed it up in these rather astonishing words. "Doing time in San Quentin was by far the hardest thing I have ever done. But it was also the best thing that ever happened to me, and I would not trade a single minute of that ordeal."[4]

INTROSPECTION.

Tell us more about what made the difference in prison, Mr. Dallas.

> [Before San Quentin] the sheer velocity at which my life moved left no time for reflection about the methods, motives, and implications of my choices. . . . A life in slow motion enabled those of us who had suffered from a lack of contemplation to come face-to-face with who we

were, who we wanted to be, who we could be, what we had done, what we could have done, and what we could do. Those are questions I should have addressed more thoughtfully before prison but instead had pushed out of my mind in the whirlwind of activity that filled my days.[5]

SIMPLICITY.

On the outside, you had what most consider the dream life with all the perks and toys possible. Don't you miss that?

After the system had restructured my existence, I was astonished to discover how little I really required to live a contented, if seemingly Spartan, life . . . . I learned to find contentment in the simple things, and as a result, I experienced a feeling of peace that was beyond my comprehension. . . . Thankfully, my frenetic-energy detox in San Quentin enabled me to become a quiet advocate for simplicity.[6]

PERSONAL FREEDOM.

OK, you had good things happen to you in prison; but still you lost your freedom. You were incarcerated in one of the most high-security prisons there is. That has to be oppressive.

But Freedom is not a physical space . . . . true freedom is all about attitude . . . . Month after month of narrowly focusing on my own situation had kept me in a prison inside the prison – the confines of my own mind. The Lifers who coached me through my sentence lacked physical freedom but had achieved personal freedom in their minds, hearts, and spirits.[7]

THE LIFERS.

"A prison inside the prison" – that takes some pondering. You mention the Lifers and that some of these inmates were valued teachers.

A few of the Lifers were clearly predators, the worst of the worst . . . but they were the exception to the rule. To my surprise, most of the Lifers had been transformed. . . . Many of us live in prisons . . . of our own making . . . . The Lifers possessed a strong hope for their own lives.[8]

These men had been sentenced to a life term, which usually lasted at least twenty years. Yet many of them seemed to take joy in helping others get their lives on track . . . and the cumulative effect was that these men gave me hope.[9]

I began hanging out with the Lifers as often as I could, eager to pick up pointers about their faith and coping skills. They became the first genuine community of faith I had ever experienced. These guys had a spiritual humility I had never witnessed before. They truly cared about me . . . . One of the most important things I noticed about the Lifers I looked up to was that, to a man, they had all given control of their lives to Christ.[10]

SPIRITUALITY - GOD.

You mention spirituality. A person typically does not associate prison with spirituality. Before prison you stated, "Religion became the heaviest burden I had yet encountered and for the next thirteen years, God was not part of the equation."[11] Now in your book, you title the introduction, "Finding God in San Quentin." Tell us about it.

At San Quentin, I finally found a church that was willing to take me in regardless of my lack of qualifications. It was the first time I had ever met people who practiced Jesus' command not to judge unless you want to be judged. . . . San Quentin dislodged my perception of the church as an institution and redefined it as a unified group of sinners who were so thrilled to be accepted by God that they accepted everyone who wanted to join them on the journey. Their emphasis was love, not rules; character, not attendance; spiritual fruit, not information retention.[12]

I had no idea at the time that my biggest issue in life was the superficiality of my character – or that the only antidote for that disease was a full-on commitment to allowing God to transform that character.[13]

For more than three decades I had tried to mature via my rules, my way. Now it was time to grow His way.[14]

FORGIVENESS.

One expects anger in prison, but you speak of forgiveness. In fact, your book has a chapter titled, "Find Freedom in Forgiveness." What do you mean?

Forgiveness was the final, critical key to my own personal transformation. In order to be truly free, I still needed to deal with the unresolved anger in my heart: anger at God, anger at the dysfunctions of my past, anger at the business world for not being what I had hoped it would be. I was angry at the system for letting me down, angry at the COs and other inmates who tried to make my life miserable, and angry at myself for the poor choices I had made.[15]

One of the most important lessons the Lifers of San Quentin taught me is this: anger toward others is a sentence more devastating than any judge could ever render. The only way we can break those shackles of anger and pain is to exercise complete and utter forgiveness.[16]

[My fellow inmate and best friend] Vy taught me and many others that when you forgive someone, the person offering forgiveness is the one who is released from bondage . . . . the prize is our own freedom.[17]

So, for you, San Quentin really was a university.

My happiness comes from knowing that this is the place where I learned to be a real man, the place where I discovered the principles that would eventually enable me to live a meaningful and successful life. I would not be the person I am today had it not been for the nurture and training I received behind those impregnable walls.[18]

Prison taught me that I am a lot tougher and stronger than I thought. That's not reflective of anything special about me; it's a statement about the untapped resilience of human beings.[19]

QUESTIONS TO PONDER AND DISCUSS:

1. What seemed most central in the turn-around of Bill Dallas?

2. What is a lesson from Bill Dallas that you could implement (or experiment with)?

3. Why did Bill Dallas consider San Quentin to be the "best thing that ever happened" to him?

A QUESTION FOR A WRITTEN ANSWER:

What is the one lesson for you to remember from Bill Dallas?

"What about the freedom of your will and spirit?"

8
James B. Stockdale, Vice Admiral
1923 – 2005

"I'm going right now from being the Wing Commander, in charge of a thousand people . . . responsible for nearly a hundred airplanes . . . to being an object of contempt. 'Criminal.'" At age 41, Commander Stockdale was shot down over North Vietnam and spent almost eight years as a prisoner of war under horrific conditions. This included four years in solitary. His conclusion: "Fetters and jail take away your external freedom. . . . But what about the freedom of your will and spirit?"[1]

> On September 9, 1965, I flew at 500 knots right into a flak trap, at treetop level, in a little A-4 airplane that I suddenly couldn't steer because it was on fire, its control system shot out. After ejection, I had about 30 seconds to make my last statement in freedom before I landed in the main street of a little village . . . . I had a broken leg (which my welcoming party, a street mob of civilians, had inflicted), a broken back . . . and a gunshot wound

in my good leg (which an irate farmer had pumped into my stretcher during my first night on the ground).[2]

EPICTETUS (EH-PEC-TEE'-TUS)

Tumbling to the ground, strapped to his parachute, Stockdale whispered to himself, "Five years down there, at least. I'm leaving the world of technology and entering the world of Epictetus." Who is Epictetus? In a later lecture to cadets, Stockdale made this unusual confession.

> It's been a one-on-one relationship. He's been in combat with me, leg irons with me, spent month-long stretches in blindfolds with me, has been in the ropes with me, has taught me that my true business is maintaining control over my moral purpose, in fact that my moral purpose is who I am. He taught me that I am totally responsible for everything I do and say; and that it is I who decides on and controls my own destruction and own deliverance.[3]

While James Stockdale was influenced by many mentors, Epictetus was his favorite. He acknowledged keeping Epictetus' writings, "on my bedside table on each of the three aircraft carriers I flew from. And I read them." It is said that Frederick the Great never went on a campaign without a copy of the words of Epictetus' small handbook, *The Enchiridion*.[4]

Epictetus (55–135 AD) was a Greek slave sold to a Roman. He achieved a superior education and was granted his freedom. He became an influential teacher, was exiled to Greece, and continued teaching. He wrote nothing, but one of his students wrote eight volumes of his words. He became a leading voice for Stoicism. James Stockdale became acquainted with Epictetus in graduate school.

TORTURE

Commander Stockdale took note of the following statements by Epictetus. First, "Adversity introduces a person to himself." And second, "Anytus and Meletus can kill me, but they can't harm me." He remembered this counsel when undergoing the worst of the tortures, "taking the ropes," which consisted of:

> Heavily slapping the prisoner, seating him on the brick floor, tying his upper arms with ropes, and while standing barefoot on his back cinching up the elaborate bindings by jerks, pulling his shoulders together while stuffing his head down between his feet with the heel of your foot. Numb arms under contorted tension produce an excruciating pain and a gnawing but sure knowledge that a clock is ticking while your blood is stopped and that the longer you wait before submitting the longer useless arms will dangle at your sides (45 minutes of blood stoppage usually costs about six months of dangle).[5]

All of Stockdale's prison associates experienced "the ropes." For Stockdale, it was 15 times. In spite of the misery inflicted, Stockdale and his associates declared their personal victory, "Each member of our 'Alcatraz Gang' won his war from a filthy cell."

YOUR BROTHER'S KEEPER

Epictetus spoke of the associates we keep. "The key is to keep company only with people who uplift you, whose presence calls forth your best." This was difficult, for prisoners were kept separate and any communication was strictly prohibited and resulted in severe punishment. Commander Stockdale was the senior officer in the prison. He knew a man left totally alone was vulnerable – that communication was vital.

In spite of the danger, "We organized a clandestine society via our wall tap code – a society with our own laws, traditions, customs, even heroes. . . . And the most important idea, as we strove to maintain our sanity, was this: *You are your brother's keeper.*"[6]

Here is an example of the encouragement provided. After a particularly grueling torture session, Stockdale returned to his cell. He was hurting and dejected. He received a signal there was a note for him.

> Back in my cell, after the guard locked the door, I sat on my toilet bucket – where I could stealthily jettison the note if the peephole cover moved – and unfolded Hatcher's sheet of low-grade paper toweling on which he had printed with rat dropping, without comment or signature, the last verse of Ernest Henley's poem 'Invictus':

> 'It matters not how strait the gate,
> How charged with punishment the scroll,
> I am the master of my fate:
> I am the captain of my soul.'[7]

SELF DISCIPLINE

Epictetus was a founding leader of the Stoic movement. Here, he states a fundamental principle of Stoicism. "Some things are up to us and some are not up to us. . . . Work with what you have control of and you'll have your hands full."[8] This is fundamental to Stoicism, Epictetus, and James Stockdale. It is essential for each person to determine the things he does not have control over and pay them no mind. But, the things under his control, he takes charge of.

> Self-discipline was vital to self-respect . . . . Self-indulgence is fatal . . . . Daily ritual seems essential to mental and spiritual health. I would do 400 pushups a day, even when I had leg irons, and would feel guilty when I failed to do them. . . . Unless [man] gets some

structure, some ritual, some poetry into his life, he is going to become an animal.[9]

CONTINUED LEARNING

There is no question – if Stockdale had been allowed books, he would have devoured them. Instead, he had to settle for "mining the memory." That is, he aroused and rekindled the association he had with authors from the past. He mentioned being encouraged by some of the mentors in this book: Dostoyevsky, Cervantes, and Solzhenitsyn. "As time wears on, ever more high-minded discourse flows from hard-worked memories which dredge up recollections of the best from the educational backgrounds of their owners."[10]

ISOLATION

Eleven men were in the prison they called Alcatraz,

> There was not a man who wound up with less than three and a half years of solitary. . . . I was alone for four and a half years. [It was Epictetus who counseled], 'Remember never to say that you are alone; for you are not alone, but God is within, and your Guardian Spirit . . . . Resolve, now if never before, to approve thyself to thyself.'[11]

Stockdale applied Epictetus' counsel.

> I didn't have anything to go on but my memories and I really sorted out the good and the bad. I fancied myself as having a practice run at growing old. If you do anything of which you are ashamed, it becomes a cancerous sore that you have to somehow accommodate in your loneliness (or in old age). But the good stuff, running the race well, will sustain you.[12]
>
> Contemplation during my years in solitary confinement led me to conclude that a good life is one that

accumulates high-quality memories. Can memories of comfort and workaday life, even a workaday life spiced with financial coups, compete with memories of bold strokes of service which one knows in his gut really mattered in the course of history?[13]

Isolation seems to have some sort of a purifying effect on the soul.[14]

SPIRITUALITY

Epictetus expressed a spiritual dimension. "Thou art thyself a fragment torn from God – thou hast a portion of Him within thyself."[15] James Stockdale expanded:

Most men need some kind of personal philosophy to endure what the Vietnam POWs endured. For many it is religion; for many it is patriotic cause; for some it is simply a question of doing their jobs. . . . Ritual fills a need in a hard life. . . . For almost all of us, this ritual was built around prayer, exercise, and clandestine communication. The prayers I said during those days were prayers of quality with ideas of substance.[16]

James Stockdale was released after almost eight years in prison as were the remaining 466 U.S. servicemen who had been captured. After 37 years of active duty, he retired from the Navy as Vice Admiral. In civilian life, he became a college president, teacher, lecturer, writer, and had brief involvement in politics. He developed and taught a course at the Naval War College titled "Foundations of Moral Obligation." One of the key principles was, "Every man can be more than he is."[17]

With any story of a prisoner is an untold story of a family. Sybil Stockdale was left to raise four children alone. She worked with other wives and helped form a national organization for families of POWs. She was credited with helping to better publicize the mistreatment of U.S. POWs. James and Sybil wrote a book together. In alternating chapters, they each told their perspective of the prison nightmare. The name of the book is, *In Love and War: The Story of a Family's Ordeal and Sacrifice During the Vietnam War.*[18]

QUESTIONS TO PONDER AND DISCUSS:

1. Summarize a central message of Epictetus.

2. Is there an Epictetus that might be a companion to you?

3. James Stockdale referred to, "Bold strokes of service which really matter." What might be a bold stroke of service that invites you?

A QUESTION FOR A WRITTEN ANSWER:

What is the one lesson for you to remember from James Stockdale?

"*Hell . . . is the suffering of being unable to love*"

9

Fyodor Dostoyevsky
1821 - 1881

Fyodor Dostoyevsky knew suffering. He was a compulsive gambler. The family business collapsed and he was so poor he sold his wedding rings and wedding presents for survival. He faced the death of his brother, his wife, a three-year old son, and a baby. And during a 20-year period he suffered 102 epileptic seizures. Yet, it wasn't these things he identified with suffering. This man, who had suffered far more than most, pronounced that it is being unable to love that is hell. His books have been translated into more than 170 languages, selling more than 15 million copies. Dostoyevsky teaches his own lessons of optimism and redemption through the characters in his books.

Fyodor Dostoyevsky was born in Moscow in 1821 to a well-to-do family. As a young man, he was a member of a secret society of liberal intellectuals who got together to discuss Western philosophy. The Tsar was fearful of any possible revolutionary talk. At age 28, Dostoyevsky was arrested as a conspirator and condemned to death. He was dressed in a death shroud in front of an open grave facing a firing squad, certain he would die. But it was a mock execution, and instead Dostoyevsky was sentenced to four years of hard labor in a Siberian work camp. His hands and feet were permanently chained until his release. When he was released, he was forced to spend five years in a military regiment. Afterward, he remained under police surveillance for the rest of his life.

Dostoyevsky's first report of his prison experience was grim.

> I once spent four hours on special emergency work when the mercury in the thermometer had frozen . . . . [In the barrack] the floor was covered in nigh on two inches of muck . . . . All the convicts stank like pigs . . . . We slept on a board plank bed and were permitted one pillow. We had to cover ourselves with our short sheep-skin coats, our legs sticking out all night uncovered. All night we shivered. There were fleas, lice and cockroach-es by the bushel.[1]

Dostoyevsky developed a profound personal philosophy, much of it from his prison life. But he didn't write about his conclusions in a normal autobiography. Instead, he wrote novels about the redemption of man – and had the lead characters speak for him.

THE HOUSE OF THE DEAD[2]

The House of the Dead is a book about life in a prison camp. A convict named Alexandr Petrovich tells the story. It appears that much of the book is autobiographical of Dostoevsky. And in the book, there is much of Dostoyevsky's familiar theme of redemption. It is about the awakening of man to his own freedom – even in captivity. Below are excerpts from the book.

A Renewed Perspective of Books

I had not read a single book for several years, and it is hard to describe the strange excitement I felt as I read my first book in prison. I remember that I began to read it one evening, after lock-up, and I went on reading all night, until daybreak. . . . I seized on every word, tried to read between the lines, tried to find hidden allusions to the life I had known.

A Changed Perspective of Other Inmates

At one point, Dostoyevsky described his prison time as "unending agony, because each hour, each minute weighed upon my soul like a stone." It took time for him to realize his prison experience had carved depth and dimension to his soul. Early, he had little appreciation for other inmates, a perspective which changed.

Even in penal servitude, among thieves and bandits, in the course of four years I finally succeeded in discovering human beings. Can you believe it: among them there are deep, strong, magnificent characters, and how cheering it was to find the gold under the course surface. And not one, not two, but several. Some, it is impossible not to respect, others are quite simply magnificent. . . . What a wonderful people. My time has not been wasted.[4]

A Changed View of Isolation

I experienced the most terrible isolation and in the end I came to cherish that isolation. Inwardly alone, I reviewed the whole of my past life, turned everything over in my mind, right down to the last detail, weighed up my past, imposed an inexorable and severe judgment on myself, and sometimes even blessed fate for having sent me such isolation, without which neither this self-judgment nor this stern review of my past life would have been possible.[5]

A Commitment to Change

What hopes did not beat within my heart in those days! I thought, I determined, I swore to myself that in my future life there would be none of those previous mistakes and lapses. I drew up a mental plan of the future and pledged myself to stick to it. Once again there rose within me a blind faith that I would fulfill this plan, that I was capable of doing so . . . I eagerly awaited my freedom, I called upon it to come quickly; I desired to put myself to the test again in a new struggle.[6]

CRIME AND PUNISHMENT[7]

Crime and Punishment is one of Dostoyevsky's best known books. The title is descriptive of the content. It is the story of a man who commits a heinous crime and gets away with it – except for his conscience. And that is the severest punishment of all.

Rodion Raskolnikov is an impoverished ex-student in St. Petersburg who devises a plan to murder and rob an unpleasant, elderly pawnbroker. Raskolnikov rationalizes that with the pawnbroker's money, he can perform good deeds that will counterbalance the crime. Plus, he will rid the world of a worthless scoundrel. He sneaks into his victim's apartment and murders her with an axe, then kills her half-sister who stumbles into the room.

But, Raskolnikov, consumed with guilt, is unable to enjoy the stolen money and acknowledges, "He had been led to the murder through his shallow and cowardly nature." Though he is not a suspect in the crime, there is still punishment. He realizes, "If [man] has a conscience he will suffer for his mistake. That will be punishment – as well as the prison."

Unable to endure the deception, Raskolnikov confesses and is given a lenient sentence of eight years of penal servitude in Siberia. His relationship with a woman is repaired and as he contemplates a new life, the last words of the book are: "But that is the beginning of a new story – the story of the gradual renewal of a man, the story of his gradual regeneration, of his passing from one world into another, of his initiation into a new unknown life."

THE BROTHERS KARAMAZOV[8]

This book was written in Dostoyevsky's final years and is regarded by many as his greatest writing. Dostoyevsky continues his central theme of redemption. He tells the story of three brothers and their father who was a drunk and a womanizer. Following are brief sketches of two of the brothers and also Father Zosima.

Father Zosima – the soldier turned monk.

Father Zosima begins as an arrogant, selfish soldier. Beating his servant for no reason catapults him into a night of self-examination, forcing him to face the meanness of his life. By morning, his whole perspective is changed. In full officer's uniform, he falls to his knees and asks forgiveness of his servant.

That morning Zosima has an appointment to fight a duel he had instigated. On his way he exclaims, "Have you ever seen a conqueror? Here is one before you." We soon find that he does not mean the conquering of another, but the conquering of a much greater adversary – himself. Rather than firing upon his opponent, he throws his loaded pistol into the woods and begs his opponent's forgiveness. He resigns his military commission, joins the monastery and becomes the much loved "Father."

In the transition, he discovers this insight.

> A man who lies to himself, and believes his own lies, becomes unable to recognize truth, either in himself or in anyone else, and he ends up losing respect for himself and for others. When he has no respect for anyone, he can no longer love, and in him, he yields to his impulses, indulges in the lowest form of pleasure, and behaves in the end like an animal in satisfying his vices. And it all comes from lying – to others and to yourself. [9]

It is Father Zosima who makes the statement, "What is hell? I maintain that it is the suffering of being unable to love."

Alyosha

Alyosha, the youngest and most spiritual Karamazov, joins the monastery. On the night of Father Zosima's death, Dostoyevsky describes Alyosha's night of enlightenment.

> His soul, filled with ecstasy . . . . He wanted to forgive all creatures for all things and to ask forgiveness. . . . A feeble youth had he fallen to the earth, yet now he arose a resolute warrior for the rest of his life and knew and felt this suddenly, at that same moment of his ecstasy. And never, never for all the rest of his life would Alyosha be able to forget that moment.[10]

Dmitri

Dmitri is the oldest of the Karamazov brothers. He is a young man committed to a life of pleasure and irresponsibility. As the story unfolds, Dmitri is wrongly charged with killing his father. He spends two months in jail awaiting trial. He is convicted of a crime he did not commit and sentenced to the labor camps. But something unexpected happens to Dmitri in jail awaiting his trial. After he is sentenced, he speaks with his brother Alyosha.

Brother, these last two months I've found in myself a new man. A new man has risen up in me. He was hidden in me, but would never have come to the surface, if it hadn't been for this blow from heaven. I am afraid! And what do I care if I spend twenty years in the mines, breaking ore with a hammer? I am not a bit afraid of that—it's something else I am afraid of now: that that new man may leave me . . . . It's all come to me here, here, within these peeling walls . . . . One cannot exist in prison without God; it's even more impossible than out of prison.[11]

Throughout his writings, we hear Dostoyevsky's beliefs through the characters in his novels.

Questions to Ponder and Discuss:

1. Comment on one of the Dostoyevsky quotes you find meaningful.

2. What is your opinion – is Dostoyevsky's redemption and transformation message realistic? If "no," why not, if "yes," to how many?

3. What does the statement mean, "Hell . . . is the suffering of being unable to love"?

A Question for a Written Answer:

What is the one lesson for you to remember from Fyodor Dostoyevsky?

*"The most extraordinary
person the human race has ever produced"*

10

Joan of Arc
1412 - 1431

It was Mark Twain who made the unusual statement about Joan of Arc found on the preceding page. It wasn't in one of Twain's humor books, it was in a biography he wrote of Joan. The biography wasn't just another of his dozens of books. He declared it was "worth all his other books together." Joan spent the last year of her life in prison and in chains. At nineteen years of age, she was burned at the stake.

During Joan's short life, what was it that led Mark Twain to make his incredible claim? Along with her inconceivable military achievements, there are at least three characteristics he observed: (1) The guidance of the inner voices, (2) her unswerving allegiance to mission, (3) her unshakeable integrity.

Joan was born in 1412 in France. She started hearing voices at about twelve years of age. The voices kept talking to her and by the time she was almost seventeen she reported receiving a divine call to rescue France.

It was a France that needed rescuing. The French population had not recovered from the Black Death. The Hundred Years' War with England had been underway almost ninety years. The English had invaded and large sections of France were under English control. A large part of France had entered into an alliance with the English. Orléans was under siege and the French army had not achieved a major victory for a generation. The economy was in ruin. The French King was deemed mad and soon died leaving the country without a crowned king. This was Joan's France.

Joan's records are still available in the National Archives of France where much of her life is documented. Following is the story Mark Twain gleaned from the records. To facilitate the story, Twain adds dialogue to the facts of history and uses Joan's page (attendant) as the story-teller.[1]

Before her 17th birthday, this is Joan's response to her calling to save France.

> But, I am so young! Oh, so young to leave my mother and my home, and go out into the strange world to undertake a thing so great! . . . How can I go to the great wars, and lead armies? – I a girl, and ignorant of such things, knowing nothing of arms, nor how to mount a horse, nor ride it ... Yet – if it is commanded – . . . God has chosen the meanest of His creatures for this work; and by His command, and in His protection, and by His strength, not mine, I am to lead His armies, and win back France, and set the crown upon the [the rightful king].[2]

Her page observed, "None who met Joan that day failed to notice the change that had come over her. She moved and spoke with energy and decision; there was a strange new fire in her eye, and also a something wholly new and remarkable in her carriage and in the set of her head."[3]

Many scoffed at Joan. But, there was something truthful and courageous about this girl, and people around the countryside came to get a glimpse of her. "And still they came, winter as it was, for when a man's soul is starving, what does he care for meat and roof so he can but get that nobler hunger fed?" The skeptical noblemen quizzed her.

> What is it that you would do? What is your hope and purpose? [Her answer] To rescue France, and it is appointed that I shall do it. For no one else in the world, neither kings, nor dukes, nor any other, can recover the kingdom of France, and there is no help but in me. . . . But indeed I would rather spin with my poor mother, for this is not my calling; but I must go and do it, for it is my Lord's will.[4]

Joan convinced the king-to-be of her mission. And then, out of desperation, the unimaginable happened. The King-in-waiting appointed Joan general-in-chief of the armies of France. She was seventeen.

Joan had an uncanny capacity to bring out the best in her soldiers. As a child, one of her young comrades was Paladin, who boasted more than he delivered. He was in her army and following is Joan's conversation with him.

> [Joan], I watched you on the road. You began badly, but improved. Of old you were a fantastic talker, but there is a man in you, and I will bring it out. Will you follow where I lead? [Answer] 'Into the fire!'

Her page observed, 'By the ring of that, I think she has turned this braggart into a hero.'[5] How does one do that – turn a braggart, or perhaps a coward, into a hero? In Joan's case, it came from focusing beyond the outward appearance into the heart – the "seeing eye."

> She has the seeing eye . . . the common eye sees only the outside of things, and judges by that, but the seeing eye pierces through and reads the heart and the soul, finding there capacities which the outside didn't indicate or promise, and which the other kind of eye couldn't detect. When a person in Joan of Arc's position tells a man

he is brave, he *believes* it; and *believing* it is enough; in fact, to believe yourself brave is to *be* brave; it is the one only essential thing.[6]

Here is another instance of the "seeing eye." A giant of a man, called The Dwarf, was brought to her as a deserter. The act was punishable by death. She saw his capacities and commanded he be spared. He responded, "I will give all my heart to you – and all my soul, if I have one – and all my strength, which is great – for I was dead and am alive again; I had nothing to live for, but now I have! You are France for me. You are my France, and I will have no other."[7]

She was bold and decisive. In command of the army, Joan of Arc rejected the cautious strategy that characterized French leadership during previous campaigns.

> From the first, we have been hindered by this policy of shilly-shally; this fashion of counseling and counseling and counseling where no counseling is needed, but only fighting. You have my orders – here and now. We will move upon the forts of the south bank tomorrow at dawn . . . . If there is but a dozen of you that are not cowards, it is enough – follow me![8]

"Shilly-shally" is a word meaning to procrastinate, vacillate, dawdle; to spend time on insignificant things. It is the opposite of decisiveness and resolve. It was the opposite of Joan.

Joan led the army in an astonishing series of victories that reversed the tide of the war. Of the Hundred Years' War, the narrator says:

> Now came the ignorant country maid out of her remote village and confronted this hoary war, this all-consuming conflagration that had swept the land for three generations. Then began the briefest and most amazing campaign that is recorded in history. In seven weeks it was

finished. In seven weeks she hopelessly crippled that gigantic war that was ninety-one years old. At Orléans she struck it a staggering blow; on the field of Patay she broke its back.[9]

Charles was officially crowned king. But then he lost the heart to vigorously pursue the war and withdrew his support. Joan did not complain, "But – she was a caged eagle just the same, and pined for the free air and the alpine heights and the fierce joys of the storm."[10] Without the support the army needed, Joan was taken prisoner in battle by the Duke of Burgundy who had accepted an alliance with England. The Duke of Burgundy waited more than five months for an expected ransom from the French king whom Joan had so diligently served. No offer came and the Duke sold Joan to the English.

> She was now shut up in the dungeons of the Castle of Rouen and kept in an iron cage with her hands and feet and neck chained to a pillar; and from that time forth during all the months of her imprisonment, till the end, several rough English soldiers stood guard over her night and day – and not outside her room, but in it. It was a dreary and hideous captivity. . . . From first to last she was a prisoner a year; and she spent the last three months of it on trial for her life before a formidable array of ecclesiastical judges.[11]

Joan was tried for heresy, witchcraft, and other offences against religion. Fifty experts, along with sixty-two judges, were against this nineteen year-old novice. They came up with seventy charges against her, later reduced to twelve. There was no one to help her. The prosecution was relentless in trying to get Joan to deny her voices and confess her wrongdoings. They asked if she still heard the voices. Her response: "They come to me every day."

Her accusers warned Joan she was speaking heresy. She was told in order to gain freedom, all she had to do was confess and deny. But Joan could not do that and maintain integrity.

> I will not say otherwise than I have said already; and if I saw the fire before me I would say it again! . . . I would rather die than be untrue to my oath to God. . . . Let come what may, here I take my stand and will abide. . . . If I were under sentence, and saw the fire before me, and the executioner ready to light it – more, if I were in the fire itself, I would say none but the things which I have said in these trials; and I would abide by them till I died.[12]

After months of coercion and duress, Joan signed a simple six-line paper. That is all her captors needed and the trap snapped shut. They attached several prepared pages to the sheet Joan had signed. Her signature was now illegally attached to a document, "confessing herself a sorceress, a dealer with devils, a liar, a blasphemer of God and His angels, a lover of blood, a promoter of sedition, cruel, wicked, commissioned of Satan."[13]

It was now an easy matter for the jury to find Joan guilty on all counts. Her judgment was inscribed upon the cap she was assigned to wear during her last hours: "HERETIC, RELAPSED, APOSTATE, IDOLATER."[14] Joan of Arc was burned at the stake.

A quarter of a century later, under the direction of the Pope, an official investigation of Joan's trial concluded that the procedure was irregular on a number of points. This prompted a "nullification trial" which declared Joan innocent of all charges. In 1920, Pope Benedict XV canonized Joan, who became one of the most popular saints of the Roman Catholic Church.

Later, Mark Twain wrote an appendix to his book including the following conclusion: "She is easily and by far the most extraordinary person the human race has ever produced."[15]

QUESTIONS TO PONDER AND DISCUSS:

1. If you had the "seeing eye," what are you likely to see in the people around you?

2. Should Joan have denied her "voices" in order to save her life? Why?

3. When you listen carefully, at your depth can *you* hear the "voices," your "better angels," urging you to a worthy mission? What is the mission?

A QUESTION FOR A WRITTEN ANSWER:

What is the one lesson for you to remember from Joan of Arc?

The liberation of self in
Cell 54

11

Anwar Sadat
1918 – 1981

It was Anwar Sadat's mission to bring about the liberation of Egypt. He found he could not do that until he liberated himself. To do that, he had to go to Cell 54 in Cairo Central Prison. He was then prepared to become president of Egypt.

Anwar Sadat tells his captivating story in his autobiography, *Anwar el-Sadat – In Search of Identity.*[1] Here is his description of his early life. "I lived below the poverty line throughout the period of my secondary school education. On his limited income, my father had to support thirteen sons and daughters."[2]

Anwar's early school success was less than exemplary. He reported the results of taking the General Certificate of Education exam. "I passed in all subjects individually, but the sum total of my marks was 'unsatisfactory.' That result was a turning point in my life . . . [With] a combined sense of guilt and a resolve to repent . . . I finally read for and obtained my GCE."[3]

At age 14, Anwar found a mentor he idolized – Mahatma Gandhi. Gandhi passed through Egypt and reports of him filled the newspapers. "I was struck by his character and fell in love with his image.

I began to imitate him." Sadat graduated from the Royal Military Academy and obtained a B.A. degree from the University of London. The other young officers he associated with would go into Cairo to play. Sadat accompanied them but, once in town, he went his own way. "I sat at a café near the railway station, smoked a hookah (pipe), and happily read the books I had bought in Cairo."

The British were in control of Egypt and Egypt's king was aligned with the British. Sadat joined a revolutionary group to fight for Egyptian freedom. The first time he was arrested, he was released. In 1942 on his second arrest, he was stripped of his military rank, sent to jail and then prison. He said he embarked on "decisive soul-searching in prison." Solitary provided him the opportunity. At Cairo Central Prison he reported, "I spent a whole year completely cut off from the outside world and was denied everything – newspapers, books, a bed, even a chair."[4]

After two years, Sadat escaped and became a fugitive. Within two years, he was arrested again for revolutionary activities and again placed in solitary confinement at Cairo Central Prison. This time, a bed, table, chair and lamp were available – if he rented them. His pursuit had been the liberation of Egypt. But before he could do that, he recognized he needed to liberate his "self." That is what he named a chapter in his book, "The Liberation of 'Self' – Cell 54." I include a number of quotes from Sadat because this time in prison had such profound and long-lasting meaning for him. How does "liberation of self" in a prison cell happen?

> In Cell 54 I could only be my own companion, day and night, and it was only natural that I should come to know that 'self' of mine. I had never had such a chance before . . . . Now in the complete solitude of Cell 54, when I had no links at all with the outside world – not even newspapers or a radio – the only way in which I could break my loneliness was, paradoxically, to seek the companionship of that inner entity I call 'self.' . . .

Nothing is more important than self-knowledge. Once
I had come to know what I wanted, and got rid of what
I didn't, I was reconciled to my 'self' and learned to live
at peace with it. . . . A person's inability to see his way
ahead makes him a prisoner within himself.[5]

One of the common ties among our mentors is that, given time to
ponder, their thoughts turn to the spiritual, to God. Anwar Sadat was
Muslim. As he contemplated the spiritual, he concluded:

The God who has created us cannot be evil in any
sense: He is good and beneficent (contrary to the image
of God which a sheikh in our village Koranic teaching school had drawn up as a mighty and frightening
Being). Ideally the relationship between man and God
should be based not on fear (or punishment and reward)
but on a much loftier value, the highest – friendship.[6]

After investigating self and God, Sadat considered his relationship
with others. I share his conclusions, which open a large window to his
soul.

My relations with the entire universe began to be re-
shaped, and love became the fountainhead of all my actions and feelings. . . . I cannot bring myself to hate
anybody, as I am by nature committed to love. This became quite clear to me through suffering and pain, in
Cell 54. Suffering crystallizes a soul's intrinsic strength;
for it is through suffering that a man of mettle can
come into his own, and fathom his own depths. It was
through suffering that I discovered how I was by nature
inclined to do good, that love was the real motivation
behind my actions. Without love I really could not work
at all. Love provided me with faith, full confidence in
myself and everything around me. . . . My paramount

object was to make people happy. To see someone smile, to feel that another man's heart beat for joy, was to me a source of immeasurable happiness. I identified with people's joys. To me love has always been a lofty human ideal, and it was in Cell 54 that I discovered that love is truly the key to everything.[7]

And as with other of our mentors, material possessions diminished in importance for Sadat.

Inside Cell 54, as my material needs grew increasingly less, the ties which had bound me to the material world began to be severed, one after another. My soul, having jettisoned its earthly freight, was freed and so took off like a bird soaring into space, into the furthest regions of existence, into infinity. So long as a man is enslaved by material needs . . . nothing will ever belong to him; he will always belong to 'things.'[8]

When the rules were eased in Cell 54, Sadat was allowed books, magazines, and newspapers. After his deprivation, they were received with celebration.

I read voraciously, finding in every word a novelty – something that opened up new horizons before my very eyes. . . . When an idea, a poem, or anything in print appealed to me, I immediately copied it into a notebook that I still keep and really cherish. I call it the Prison Notebook. It includes quotations from world authors – Eastern and Western alike – who have had a marked influence on my life. . . . [Further, with restrictions eased], I walked 2-1/2 miles every morning, and still do.[9]

Overjoyed at what he was accomplishing, Anwar Sadat summarized his prison lessons in an astonishing way.

Once released from the narrow confines of the 'self,' with its mundane suffering and petty emotions, a man will have stepped into a new, undiscovered world which is vaster and richer. His soul would enjoy absolute freedom . . . . This is why I regard my last eight months in prison as the happiest period in my life. . . . This could never have happened if I had not had such solitude as enabled me to recognize my real self.[10]

After three years, Sadat was brought to trial. If the revolutionary charges could be proved, the sentence would be death or hard labor for life. But, charges were not proved. He was declared not guilty and released. Anwar Sadat was a free man after spending an uninterrupted thirty-six months in prison. He was reinstated in the armed forces with the rank of captain and soon promoted to lieutenant colonel.

British domination and the Egyptian King were ousted after 75 years of British occupation. Gamal Abdel Nasser became president of Egypt. But, Nasser's presidency was not a happy one. Sadat provided this description, "Nasser...always left a trail of hatred." Nassar appointed Sadat as his vice-president, and after Nassar died in 1970, Anwar Sadat was elected president of Egypt.

Egypt was in shambles. Nasser had ruled the people with fear. Anyone disagreeing with the official line of thinking was arrested. The revolution Sadat had helped bring about "was reduced to a huge, dark, and terrible pit, inspiring fear and hatred but allowing no escape." The economy was a wreck. Foreign policy was virtually nonexistent, as the only international relationship that existed was with one nation, the Soviet Union. In Cairo, Soviet agents began their power struggle. The U.S. envoy who visited Egypt returned home and reported to President Nixon that Sadat wouldn't survive in power more than four or six weeks. Sadat was known as Nasser's flunky, or poodle.

Few really knew of Anwar Sadat's personal power honed in Cell 54. But, Anwar Sadat knew.

I was accepting that burden – that nightmare with all its vast dimensions – because I believed that I could do something about it. . . . I knew that this also meant I should have to challenge many conditions and ethical codes in existence at the time; but I believed I had the capacity for this. Indeed, due to the inner power I always felt, I had never been afraid to challenge existing conditions . . . . This was my forte, and I proceed from the ideals I had always adopted, inspired by my love of Egypt and my desire to make the country a happy one. Never had I had a better chance of putting my principles into practice.[11]

Sadat launched another war with Israel which regained the land Egypt had lost during the six-day war. Sadat wanted peace with Israel but believed it could only be negotiated from a position of strength, not weakness. From that position, after the war, Sadat boldly initiated the most stunning move of all – he initiated the peace process with Israel.

It was then that I drew, almost unconsciously, on the inner strength I had developed in Cell 54 of Cairo Central Prison – a strength, call it a talent or capacity, for change. I found that I faced a highly complex situation, and that I couldn't hope to change it until I had armed myself with the necessary psychological and intellectual capacity. My contemplation of life and human nature in that secluded place had taught me that he who cannot change the very fabric of his thought will never be able to change reality, and will never, therefore, make any progress.[12]

Sadat initiated dialog with Israel and when Prime Minister Begin agreed to a visit, Sadat said, "That's excellent. We'll announce it. Everybody in my government will be against it, but I know it's right." On November 20, 1977, he was in Israel and spoke to the Israeli Knesset saying, "Why don't we stand together with the courage of men and the boldness of heroes who dedicate themselves to a sublime aim?"[13]

Egypt and Israel signed a historic peace treaty. Sadat was honored as Time magazine's "Man of the Year." He was awarded the Nobel Peace Prize. But, there were those who were unhappy. October 6, 1981, after serving as Egyptian president eleven years, Anwar Sadat was assassinated during an annual victory parade. The assassination was enacted by members of the Egyptian Islāmic Jihad who accused Sadat of religious apostasy and condemned him for the peace treaty with Israel.

Early, U.S. Secretary of State, Henry Kissinger judged Sadat to be a "second-rater." He later acknowledged that to have been one of his greatest miscalculations. He stated, "Great men are so rare that they take some getting used to."

QUESTIONS TO PONDER AND DISCUSS:

1. In your opinion, what was central in Sadat becoming a successful leader?

2. Why did Sadat say, "I regard my last eight months in prison as the happiest period in my life?"

3. Can *you* have a "Cell 54" experience? If "no," why not? If "yes," how?

A QUESTION FOR A WRITTEN ANSWER:

What is the one lesson for you to remember from Anwar Sadat?

The reality of fiction

12

Jean Valjean
1802 - 1885 (Victor Hugo)

Les Miserables[1] is a book of fiction and Jean Valjean is a fictional character. Why has this work been celebrated more than 150 years? Why has it inspired a spectacularly popular play and movie? Perhaps it is as Victor Hugo said of his book: "[It is] a progress from evil to good, from injustice to justice, from falsehood to truth, from night to day . . . from hell to heaven, from nothingness to God." Perhaps in our hearts, we want that for us.

Victor Hugo did not serve prison time though he did spend fifteen years in political exile. During this time he wrote *Les Miserables*, the story of one of the world's most famous prisoners – Jean Valjean (pronounced John Valjohn). It is perhaps literature's most heartening story of a prisoner's redemption and transformation. It is fiction, but the question is, can it be reality, should it be reality?

The setting of the story is France in the early 1800s. Jean Valjean lost his parents when he was very young. He was raised by his older sister, a widow with seven young children. When he was old enough, Jean supported the family. Times were hard and the family often had little or nothing to eat. After stealing a loaf of bread for the family, Jean was caught, convicted, and sentenced to five years in prison. Jean had time to reflect on his life.

> Human society had done him nothing but injury; never had he seen anything of her but the wrathful face she calls justice, when showing it to those she strikes down. No man had ever touched him except to bruise him. All his contact with men had been by blows. Never, since infancy, since his mother, since his sister, never had he been greeted with a friendly word or a kind look. Through suffering upon suffering he gradually came to the conclusion that life is a war and that in that war he was the vanquished. He had no weapon but his hatred.[2]

Jean made several attempts to escape from prison which only added years to his sentence. Finally, after nineteen years, he was freed from the galleys, but within he was still imprisoned.

> Jean Valjean entered the galleys sobbing and trembling; he left hardened. He entered in despair; he left sullen. What had happened within this soul? . . . Under the whip, under the chain, in the cell, in fatigue, under the searing sun of the galleys, on the convict's plank bed, he turned inward to his own conscience, and he thought things over . . . he condemned society and sentenced it. He sentenced it to his hatred.[3]

Upon his release, Valjean was compelled to carry a passport identifying himself as a criminal and was required to show it wherever he went. His passport had a special notation, "A very dangerous man." Upon his release, he walked to Digne, a nearby town, and showed his identification papers to city officials as required. Though he had money from his prison work, no one would provide him food or lodging – no one except the bishop, Monseigneur Bienvenu.

The bishop is central in the story of Valjean. Note this intriguing description, "He did not study God; he was dazzled by him." How does one do that; what was his secret?

> It seemed as though it were a sort of rite with him, to prepare himself for sleep by meditating in the presence of the great spectacle of the starry firmament . . . . He was there alone with himself. . . . opening his soul to the thoughts that fall from the Unknown ... expanding his soul in ecstasy ... he felt something floating away from him, and something descending upon him . . . .[4]

The bishop gave Valjean a meal, a bed, and kindness. But Jean Valjean, hardened after nineteen years of imprisonment, was unable to accept kindness. After sleeping a few hours, he arose very early in the morning, stole the bishop's silverware and ran. He was apprehended by the authorities, brought back to the bishop's for recognition, condemnation, and another prison sentence. Instead, the bishop had him released and gave him more – his precious silver candlesticks too, the last thing of monetary value in the house. But, there was a price the old bishop expected, "Do not forget, ever, that you have promised me to use this silver to become an honest man." Jean Valjean, who had no recollection of any such promise, stood dumbfounded. The bishop continued, solemnly, "Jean Valjean, my brother, you no longer belong to evil, but to good. It is your soul I am buying for you. I withdraw it from dark thoughts and from the spirit of perdition, and I give it to God!"[5]

Confused, Jean Valjean was free to go. Later in the day, he encountered a boy and stole a small coin from the lad. Then, suddenly aware of what he had done, he frantically tried to find the boy, without success.

> His knees suddenly bent under him, as if an invisible power suddenly overwhelmed him with the weight of his bad conscience; he fell exhausted onto a large rock, his hands clenched in his hair, and his face on his knees,

and cried out, 'I'm such a miserable man!' Then his heart swelled, and he burst into tears. It was the first time he had wept in nineteen years.[6]

THE TRANSFORMATION OF JEAN VALJEAN

Rarely are we allowed to view the soul of a man struggling between light and darkness, between angels and demons. The next paragraphs, directly from Victor Hugo, reveal the sacred process.

When Jean Valjean left the bishop's house, as we saw, his thoughts were unlike any he had ever known before. He could understand nothing of what was going on inside him. He stubbornly resisted the angelic deeds and the gentle words of the old man . . . his hardness of heart could be complete, if it resisted this kindness.[7]

While he wept, the light grew brighter and brighter in his mind – an extraordinary light, a light at once entrancing and terrible. His past life, his first offense, his long expiation, his exterior degradation, his interior hardening . . . what had happened to him at the bishop's . . . all this returned and appeared to him, clearly, but in a light he had never seen before. He could see his life, and it seemed horrible; his soul, and it seemed frightful. There was, however, a gentler light shining on that life and soul. It seemed to him that he was looking at Satan by the light of Paradise.[8]

FATHER MADELEINE

The struggle lasted through the night and by dawn, an immense change had taken place in Jean Valjean. He had abandoned his hatred, he had accepted peace. He had rejected darkness, he emanated light. He then discarded his name, he settled in a small town, Montreuil-sur-mer, as a mysterious stranger. He invented a new manufacturing method and set up a manufacturing plant that made him and the town rich. He spent more than a million francs to improve the city and care for the poor.

> It seemed that he thought a lot about others, and little about himself. . . . The area owed a great deal to this man, the poor owed him everything; he was so honest that everyone finally had to respect him, and so kind that no one could help loving him; his workmen in particular adored him.[9]

At first he was known as Father Madeleine, then to confer greater respect it became Monsieur Madeleine. Then, at the insistence of the king and the people, he became Monsieur the Mayor.

But always there was the closely held secret – he had broken parole and was still a convict. And one day, he received news that another ex-convict was identified as Jean Valjean, and the man was about to be sentenced to prison in Valjean's place. The test began, and Jean Valjean had a choice to make. An innocent man was being sent to prison in his place. Could he remain in his comfortable life where he was doing much good and let an innocent man take his place in prison? Or, must he leave the life he had built, free the innocent man, and go back to prison himself? Jean Valjean agonized, and total integrity won. He went to the court and confessed, and in the drama of the moment, he walked out. For the rest of his life, he left the role of Father Madeleine the Mayor and became a fugitive evading the law.

FONTAINE, COSETTE, MARIUS

In the meantime, an unmarried girl named Fontaine gave birth to a baby girl. She and her baby Cosette were abandoned and left in a situation holding great stigma. To look for work, Fontaine left her little girl with an unscrupulous couple who owned an inn. She found employment in Jean Valjean's factory and sent money for the care of Cosette. Unbeknown to Valjean, Fontaine was mistreated and lost her job. To continue paying the outrageous demands of those caring for Cosette, the frantic mother resorted to selling her hair, her teeth, and her soul. When Valjean learned of Fontaine's plight, he cared for her and before she died, promised he would find and care for Cosette.

Jean Valjean found the mistreated Cosette and took her with him. "The bishop had caused the dawn of virtue on his horizon; Cosette evoked the dawn of love." For ten years, while avoiding the law, they were father and daughter. And then, as happens to beautiful young women, she fell in love, and she married Marius. Valjean confessed to Marius that he was a convict, still wanted by the law. Marius had difficulty accepting Valjean's convict status and Jean Valjean was alone as an old man.

By chance, Marius discovered part of the heroic past of Jean Valjean – his integrity, his valor, his commitment to good – and his service to Marius. As he realized the true character of the man, Marius and Cosette rushed to see the ailing Valjean. They found him on his deathbed. Jean Valjean's last words give evidence of the totality and finality of his transformation.

> 'I shall die in a few minutes . . . . Come closer . . . both
> of you. . . . So I am going away, my children. Love each
> other dearly always. There is scarcely anything else in
> the world but that: to love one another . . . . I see a light.
> Come nearer. I die happy.'[10]

QUESTIONS TO PONDER AND DISCUSS:

1. Is it possible you have already encountered the kindness of a "bishop" – but have rejected or forgotten?

2. At what level are you in the Jean Valjean inner struggle for transformation?

> a- Haven't had it yet.
> b- In the middle of it.

c- Been through it, resolved, relapsed.

d- Been through it, resolved, maintained.

3. Is someone waiting for you to be the "bishop" to them?

A QUESTION FOR A WRITTEN ANSWER:

What is the one lesson for you to remember from Jean Valjean?

A conversation in solitary

13
Boethius
480 – 526 AD

How does a man achieve consolation in solitary confinement – no one to talk with, no books, no hope of release? The question intensifies when the man has had great wealth, a reputation for immense intellect and integrity, and has been Roman Consul – the highest office in the Roman government. Moreover, what if he was wrongly accused and condemned to death? How does such a one achieve consolation?

Boethius (Bo-ee'thee-us) was born in Rome about 480 AD. In his early forties and at the peak of exceptional power and fortune, he defended a Roman senator who had been unjustly accused. The senator had enemies and Boethius was charged with treason and sacrilege. He was imprisoned, his wealth was confiscated, and his library destroyed. He was executed at age 46.

Boethius left a gift – a record of a conversation he had in his cell with a spiritual guide. For hundreds of years his book was the most widely copied non-religious book in Europe. It has been described as "by far the most interesting example of prison literature the world has ever seen." His book, *The Consolation of Philosophy*,[1] is ours fifteen hundred years after it was written.

As Boethius lamented the tragedy of his circumstance, he tells us he was visited by a majestic woman named Lady Philosophy. Today, the term philosophy typically refers to an academic discipline. In Boethius's day, philosophy meant the love and pursuit of *wisdom*. Since the term *wisdom* seems to communicate most accurately Boethius's experience, I will take the liberty of calling his visitor Lady Wisdom. A fascinating conversation takes place between Boethius and his visitor.

Boethius: "While I silently pondered these things, and decided to write down my wretched complaint, there appeared standing above me a woman of majestic countenance whose flashing eyes seemed wise beyond the ordinary wisdom of men."

Lady Wisdom: "It is time for medicine rather than complaint. . . . You have forgotten yourself a little."[2]

Boethius:
"There is now no hope for freedom of any kind . . . surely I did not deserve . . . . I defended the innocence of the whole Senate . . . instead of being rewarded for true virtue, I am falsely punished as a criminal. . . . Well, here am I, stripped of my possessions and honors, my reputation ruined, punished because I tried to do good."[3]

Lady Wisdom:
I am not so much disturbed by this prison as by your attitude . . . . Now, I know another cause of your sickness, and the most important: you have forgotten what you are. And so I am fully aware of the reason for your sickness and the remedy for it too. You are confused because you have forgotten what you are. . . . You have the best

medicine for your health in your grasp of the truth . . . .
Therefore, you have nothing to fear. From this tiny
spark, the living fire can be rekindled.[4]

The problem was not the imprisonment of his body, but his mind.
The primary message of Lady Wisdom was, *you have forgotten yourself
. . . you have forgotten what you are.* Boethius had not only forgotten
who he was, but *what* he was. It appears he had forgotten the capacity
and resilience embedded in man. He had forgotten the power residing
within to deal with even the most severe challenge. And then Lady
Wisdom describes the remedy – *truth*: *From this tiny spark, the living
fire can be rekindled.*

Another woman enters the conversation by the name of *Fortune* –
the capricious goddess of temporal prosperity whose allegiance has
caused Boethius's suffering. Today, we might call her Lady Luck or
perhaps Chance. Lady Wisdom points out the impending disaster
when one relies on fortune, luck, or chance as opposed to relying on
wisdom.

Lady Wisdom:
> You are wrong if you think that Fortune has changed
> toward you. This is her nature, the way she always be-
> haves. She is changeable, and so in her relations with
> you she has merely done what she always does . . . . For
> now she has deserted you, and no man can ever be se-
> cure until he has been forsaken by Fortune.[5]

The invitation of goddess Fortune is opposite that of Lady Wisdom.
Fortune is external, fickle, frivolous, and temporal. Pleasure is paramount. It is luck and chance. It is possession. Boethius had difficulty
escaping the thoughts of Fortune – she was so beautiful and intriguing.
His musings were interrupted by Lady Wisdom.

Lady Wisdom:

> Why then do men look outside themselves for happiness which is within? Money is more precious when it is generously got rid of . . . . For nature's needs are few and small; if you try to glut yourself with too many things, you will find your excesses either unpleasant or positively harmful. . . . I suppose you are trying to avoid poverty by acquiring possessions. But you will find just the opposite: you will need more in order to keep the various valuable things you have. Those who have much, need much; and, on the contrary, those who limit their possessions to their natural needs, rather than to their excessive ambitions, need very little. Do you try to satisfy your desires with external goods which are foreign to you because you have no good within you which belongs to you?[6]

Painful counsel! It is easy and seemingly natural to crave an abundance of what so many others have. It is the need for *more*. Lady Wisdom says a focus on the external means ignoring one's inner wealth. It means giving up freedom. It means focusing on the superficial and abandoning one's *self*. And how much pondering can be done on the counsel: *Money is more precious when it is generously got rid of*?

Boethius raised another issue – he missed the admiration of his friends. Again there was an answer.

Lady Wisdom: "You mortals, however, know how to act justly only when you have the support of popular opinion and empty rumor; you are not satisfied with the assurance of conscience and virtue but seek your reward in the hollow praise of other men."[7]

How easy it is to take an opinion poll of associates and adopt their standards, especially when given praise for doing so. But there is a remedy – one's own *conscience and virtue*.

As Boethius continued to lament his suffering, Lady Wisdom admonished him to adopt a different view.

Lady Wisdom:

> I am convinced that adverse fortune is more beneficial to men than prosperous fortune. . . . Good fortune deceives, adverse fortune teaches . . . good fortune seduces weak men away from the true good through flattery; but misfortune often turns them around and forcibly leads them back to the true good. . . . . You will find what I have yet to say bitter to the taste, but, once you have digested it, it will seem sweet.[8]

Boethius is told it is *adverse* fortune which expands the soul! She encourages him to redirect his focus to his inner spirit and find its treasures – unopened gifts awaiting discovery.

Lady Wisdom: "Man . . . must turn the light of his inner vision upon himself. He must guide his soaring thoughts back again and teach his spirit that it possesses hidden among its own treasures whatever it seeks outside itelf."[9]

But all Lady Wisdom has spoken is preliminary to this culminating idea – the secret of happiness.

Lady Wisdom:

> Since men become happy by acquiring happiness, and since happiness is divinity itself, it follows that men become happy by acquiring divinity. For as men become just by acquiring integrity, and wise by acquiring wisdom, so they must in a similar way become gods by acquiring divinity. Thus everyone who is happy is a god.[10]

Stunning! Lady Wisdom is saying happiness is divinity. Rather than pursuing happiness directly, one is to seek divinity. And acquiring divinity brings, not only happiness, but godliness.

And at last, Boethius understood.

Boethius: "And I am at last shamed of the folly that so profoundly depressed me . . . although the sorrow caused by my misfortunes had made me forget these truths, I had not always been ignorant of them."[11]

Boethius acknowledged he had abandoned Self and had forgotten the truths he had once known. His task was to remember what he already most deeply knew – but had forgotten.

QUESTIONS TO PONDER AND DISCUSS:

1. What have *you* forgotten that you once knew or promised?

2. What does Lady Wisdom mean when she said, "men become happy by acquiring divinity"?

3. What is *your* Lady Wisdom trying to tell *you*?

A QUESTION FOR A WRITTEN ANSWER:

What is the one lesson for you to remember from Boethius?

"Who am i? They mock me, these lonely questions of mine."

14

Dietrich Bonhoeffer

1906 - 1945

"Who am I?" is the central question we all face. Prison seems to amplify its priority. Dietrich Bonhoeffer denounced Hitler during the tumultuous years in Germany leading to World War II. It was a defiance that cost him his life.

Dietrich Bonhoeffer graduated with a doctoral degree in theology from the University of Berlin, achieving highest honors. Two days after Hitler was installed as Chancellor, Bonhoeffer delivered a radio address in which he attacked Hitler and warned Germany against their new leader. He was cut off the air in mid sentence. That was the beginning of his dangerous activity with the German resistance movement.

Bonhoeffer visited the United States where he was urged by friends to stay and be safe. But, he returned to Germany saying,

> I have come to the conclusion that I made a mistake
> in coming to America. I must live through this dif-
> ficult period in our national history with the people
> of Germany. I will have no right to participate in
> the reconstruction of Christian life in Germany

after the war if I do not share the trials of this time with my people.

He returned to Germany on the last scheduled steamer to cross the Atlantic. Fully aware of the danger involved, he said on the ship his spirit became quiet because he knew that he was doing what he was destined to do.

Back in Germany, Bonhoeffer recommitted to the resistance movement, including plotting the assassination of Hitler. He was arrested April 5, 1943. After two years imprisonment, without a trial, Bonhoeffer was stripped of his clothes and led into the execution yard where he was hanged. He was 39 years old. He died just 23 days before the German surrender. His grave has not been found.

Love and a relationship with a woman came late for Dietrich Bonhoeffer. Soon before his imprisonment at age 37, he finally became engaged to be married. He longed to be a father. He felt a calling to help Christianity be more practical. He had a zeal for life. Yet he chose the road of imminent danger. There are so many questions to ask such a man. Fortunately his writing has been compiled into a book: *Letters & Papers from Prison*.[1]

The book begins with some of Bonhoeffer's writings on New Year's Day 1943, three months before he was arrested. He used writing to clarify his thoughts and prepare his soul for the inevitable challenges ahead. Here are three excerpts that reveal much about Mr. Bonhoeffer.

> Time lost is time in which we have failed to live a full human life, gain experience, learn, create, enjoy, and suffer; it is time that has not been filled up, but left empty.[2]

> The only profitable relationship to others – and especially to our weaker brethren – is one of love.[3]

> I believe that God can and will bring good out of evil, even out of the greatest evil. For that purpose he needs men who make the best use of everything.[4]

Three months later, Bonhoeffer was arrested and imprisoned. Charges were not filed; there was not a trial. All he had were his thoughts, his compassion, and his ability to write letters. Fortunately, he gained the respect of his guards so that some of them smuggled out his papers and poems, even apologizing for having to lock his door.

Below are excerpts from his prison letters, arranged by general topic. I precede each with a question I would like to have asked this remarkable man had I been able to interview him.

MAINTAINING SANITY

Dr. Bonhoeffer, you have been a very active, energized man. How do you manage to keep sane in the confinement of prison?

I read, meditate, write, pace up and down my cell. The great thing is to stick to what one still has and can do – there is still plenty left – and not to be dominated by the thought of what one cannot do, and by feelings of resentment and discontent.[5]

I heard someone say yesterday that the last years had been completely wasted as far as he was concerned. I'm very glad that I have never yet had that feeling, even for a moment.[6]

It often seems hard to have to spend the beautiful long summer days here for the second time; but one just can't choose where one has to be. So we must keep on trying to find our way through the petty thoughts that irritate us, to the great thoughts that strengthen us.[7]

POSSESSIONS

You weren't wealthy in the life you previously led, but you had plenty for your needs. One wonders how difficult was it to leave all that behind? It seems the answer is in a letter you sent your mother regarding your possessions.

Prison life in general brings one back, both outwardly and inwardly, to the simplest things of life.[8]

In short, give away whatever anyone might need, and don't give it another thought . . . . The last two years have taught me how little we can get along with . . . . When one thinks how many people lose everything each day, one really has no claim on possessions of any kind.[9]

SOLITUDE

You are a gregarious man closely involved with the members of your church congregation. How are you doing in solitary?

When the bells rang this morning, I longed to go to church, but instead I did as John did on the island of Patmos, and had such a splendid service of my own, that I did not feel lonely at all, for you were all with me, every one of you, and so were the congregations in whose company I have kept.[10]

I've come to love solitude. I very much like to talk with two or three people, but I detest anything like a large assembly, and above all any chatter or gossip.[11]

I've got so used to the silence of solitude by now that after a short time I long for it again.

You need to get right down to fundamentals, to come to terms with life, and for that you need plenty of time to yourself.[12]

TURBULENCE

Throughout most of your years, there has been a good deal of tranquility to your life. Now, your life is filled with turmoil and hardship. Don't you resent having to live in such distressing times?

I can only say that I have no wish to live in any other time than our own, even though it is so inconsiderate of our outward well-being.[13]

One gradually learns to acquire an inner detachment from life's menaces.[14]

You must never doubt I'm travelling with gratitude and cheerfulness along the road where I'm being led. My past life is brim-full of God's goodness.[15]

LIVING IN DANGER

Many say it is likely you will not survive, that the Gestapo will kill you. How can you stay peaceful?

But at the same time we must think about things much more important to us than life itself. When the alert [air raid siren] goes, for instance: as soon as we turn our minds from worrying about our own safety to the task of helping other people to keep calm, the situation is completely changed.[16]

A POEM – WHO AM I?

Dr. Bonhoeffer, what have you learned about yourself in prison? You seem so composed and calm. Is that really how you feel? You wrote a poem about who you are. Will you share parts of it? Who is Dietrich Bonhoeffer?

Who am I? They often tell me
I stepped from my cell's confinement
Calmly, cheerfully, firmly.
Who am I? They also tell me
I bore the days of misfortune
Equably, smilingly, proudly,
Like one accustomed to win.
Am I then really that which other men tell of?
Or am I only what I myself know of myself?
Restless and longing and sick, like a bird in a cage,
Struggling for breath, as though hands were compressing my
throat,

Yearning for colors, for flowers, for the voices of birds,
Thirsting for words of kindness, for neighborliness,
Powerlessly trembling for friends at an infinite distance,
Weary and empty at praying, at thinking, at making,
Faint, and ready to say farewell to it all.
Who am I? This or the Other?
Am I one person to-day and to-morrow another?
Am I both at once? . . .
Who am I? They mock me, these lonely questions of mine.
Whoever I am, Thou knowest, O God, I am thine![17]

QUESTIONS TO PONDER AND DISCUSS:

1. Was it worth it for Dietrich Bonhoeffer to give up safety in America for what resulted in his death?

2. Select one of Bonhoeffer's quotations that is meaningful to you and explain why.

3. Who are *you?*

A QUESTION FOR A WRITTEN ANSWER:

What is the one lesson for you to remember from Deitrich Bonhoeffer?

The maddest wise man or the wisest mad man

15

Miguel de Cervantes
1547 - 1616

By most any standard, the Spaniard Miguel de Cervantes lived a life filled with challenges. This included being in prison at least three times, perhaps five. Yet, he wrote what many consider to be the world's greatest novel, later made into a popular musical and movie.

As a young soldier, in the famed Battle of Lepanto, Cervantes received three gunshot wounds – one to the chest and another to an arm, leaving it permanently useless. He was captured by pirates and sold to the Moors as a slave. After five years, he was ransomed by his parents with the help of a church group. He had been unsuccessful as a playwright. For "offenses against His Majesty's Most Catholic Church," he had been excommunicated. As a tax collector, discrepancies were found in his records, for which he spent time in jail. Through most of his life, it appears he was broke.

Cervantes arrived back in jail at age fifty-seven. As he searched his soul, he nevertheless found idealism, honor, chivalry, and humor – along with a touch of madness. Regarding his useless left arm, he said he had "lost the movement of the left hand for the glory of the right," meaning he could still write. Our knowledge of this man's life is limited. But, what we do know, in spite of his personal and prison misfortunes, there was something inside him clamoring for release. In prison, Miguel de Cervantes began to write. The result was *Don Quixote*,[1] a story of the misadventures of a mad knight errant.

The book became popular almost immediately, a popularity which continues to expand after four hundred years. *Encyclopedia Britannica* designated *Don Quixote* as one of the "Great Books of the Western World." One of our mentors, Fyodor Dostoevsky called it "the ultimate and most sublime work on human thinking."

There is little information about Cervantes' prison experience, but there are volumes describing his memorable legacy that has inspired millions. This includes Dale Wasserman who wrote the internationally acclaimed musical play, *Man of La Mancha*,[2] the story of Don Quixote. Further, *Man of La Mancha* was made into a major Hollywood movie.

Two factors justify an inclusion of Miguel de Cervantes as one of our prison mentors. First is Cervantes himself – a down-and-out "jail-bird," who contributed a lasting legacy to millions. Second, the message in the book, the play, and the music it inspired, is a testament to the resilience and possibilities of mankind, incarcerated or not.

Don Quixote is often thought to be partially autobiographical of Cervantes himself. The story begins with Alonzo Quixana – an elderly gentleman whose prized possessions are his books. He becomes interested, then obsessed, with knights and tales of chivalry. As an old man, he has a passion to become a knight errant, travel the world with horse and armor in search of adventure, and redress all manner of wrongs. While most only dream of such things, Alonzo Quixana takes the name of Don Quixote, dresses in makeshift knight garb, and persuades his neighbor Sancho to accompany him as his squire. "He was spurred on by the conviction that the world needed his immediate presence." The book is a thousand page story of his misadventures – both touching and amusing.

Every knight errant must have a Lady. From a farm girl he had met, Don Quixote invents his Lady Dulcinea, who exists only in his mind.

Yet this woman of perfect beauty and virtue serves as the inspiration of his chivalrous deeds.

There is a strange mixture in Don Quixote of sanity and madness as in his declaration, "Too much sanity may be madness and the maddest of all, to see life as it is and not as it should be." For all the madness, following are two statements of Don Quixote describing life as it should be.

> Remember that there are two kinds of beauty: one of the soul and the other of the body. That of the soul displays its radiance in intelligence, in chastity, in good conduct, in generosity, and in good breeding, and all these qualities may exist in an ugly man. And when we focus our attention upon that beauty, not upon the physical, love generally arises with great violence and intensity.

> It is not the responsibility of knights errant to discover whether the afflicted, the enchained and the oppressed whom they encounter on the road are reduced to these circumstances and suffer this distress for their vices, or for their virtues: the knight's sole responsibility is to succor them as people in need, having eyes only for their sufferings, not for their misdeeds.[3]

Don Quixote's misadventures include battling a windmill, mistaking an inn for a castle, and attacking a heard of sheep. But the encounters take their toll on our knight. Finally, Don Quixote acknowledges, "Truly I was born to be an example of misfortune, and a target at which the arrows of adversary are aimed." He returns home broken in spirit and is put to bed. He again acknowledged his name is Alonso Quixana and he denounces chivalry and knighthood.

That was the end of the book but not the end of the story. Dale Wasserman wrote *Man of La Mancha* as a "way of paying tribute to the tough and tender spirit of Miguel de Cervantes," In the play, two themes are highlighted. One is Aldonza, a harlot in whom Quixote sees majesty and to whom he refers as his Lady Dulcinea. The other theme is The Quest.

As previously stated, the book ends with Don Quixote resuming his former life as Alonzo Quixana. He is tired, without his dream or any memory of it, and is ready to die. In *Man of La Mancha*, the uninvited Aldonza and Sancho come to visit. Because Don Quixote had seen the hidden majesty in her, Aldonza is a transformed woman. She is no longer Aldonza, but Dulcinea. "You spoke to me and everything was – different! And you looked at me! And you called me by another name! Won't you please bring back the dream of Dulcinea."[4]

Slowly, Don Quixote remembers the words. As a dying man, his last act, with Sancho and Dulcinea, is to sing "The Impossible Dream."

> To dream the impossible dream,
> To fight the unbeatable foe,
> To bear with unbearable sorrow
> To run where the brave dare not go;
> To right the unrightable wrong.
>
> To love, pure and chaste, from afar,
> To try, when your arms are too weary,
> To reach the unreachable star!
> This is my Quest to follow that star,
> No matter how hopeless, no matter how far,
> To fight for the right
> Without question or pause,
> To be willing to march into hell
> For a heavenly cause!
>
> And I know, if I'll only be true
> To this glorious Quest,
> That my heart will lie peaceful and calm
> When I'm laid to my rest.

And the world will be better for this,
That one man, scorned and covered with scars,
Still strove, with his last ounce of courage,
To reach the unreachable star![5]

It seems we all have a dream – to march through our own hell in pursuit of The Quest – leaving some good in the world that outlasts our lives, to know we made a difference.

QUESTIONS TO PONDER AND DISCUSS:

1. What if, rather than inspiring millions, Cervantes writing only inspired a half-dozen family members, or maybe only one. Would it have been worth it?

2. Comment on a part in "The Impossible Dream" song that is most memorable to you.

3. What is *your* Quest, *your* Impossible Dream (or at least improbably dream)?

A QUESTION FOR A WRITTEN ANSWER:

What is the one lesson for you to remember from Miguel de Cervantes?

Anarchist to advocate

16

Eldridge Cleaver
1935 - 1998

Eldridge Cleaver went from atheist to born-again Christian. He went from a Black Panther Marxist to a born-again Republican. He went from *Soul on Ice*[1] to *Soul on Fire*.[2] What happened?

His beginning was less than exemplary. Born in 1935, he was raised in California by an abusive father and a mother who was a janitor at his junior high school. At age thirteen he started smoking marijuana, was arrested for bicycle theft, and sent to reform school. After his release, he was sent back to reform school for selling marijuana. A few days after this release, he was arrested for possession of marijuana and sentenced to two-and-one-half years at Soledad State Prison. After that term was up, he was convicted of rape and assault with intent to murder. By the time he was twenty, he was incarcerated in Folsom Prison, then transferred to San Quentin.

What did prison do to Eldridge Cleaver? It wasn't good.

> I was soon aflame with indignation . . . and inwardly
> I turned away from America with horror, disgust and
> outrage. . . . I had come to believe that there is no God
> . . . all religions were phony . . . I was an 'outlaw.' I had

stepped outside of the white man's law, which I repudiated with scorn and self-satisfaction. I became a law unto myself – my own legislature, my own supreme court, my own executive.[3]

Further encounters with the law were predictable. Upon his release, Cleaver became a rapist, involved in a shoot-out with police, was apprehended and returned to prison. This time, introspection brought penetrating analysis.

After I returned to prison, I took a long look at myself and, for the first time in my life, admitted that I was wrong, that I had gone astray – astray not so much from the white man's law as from being human, civilized – for I could not approve the act of rape. Even though I had some insight into my own motivations, I did not feel justified. I lost my self-respect. My pride as a man dissolved and my whole fragile moral structure seemed to collapse, completely shattered. . . . That is why I started to write. To save myself. I realized that no one could save me but myself.[4]

In his writings, Eldridge Cleaver comes across as an exceptionally bright, educated man. However, though intelligent, he was not school-educated. During this prison stay, Cleaver went from San Quentin back to Folsom and solitary confinement for being an agitator. Following is a clue to his education: "I had evolved a crash program which I would immediately activate whenever I was placed in solitary: stock up on books and read, read, read; do calisthenics and forget about the rest of the world."[5]

Soul on Ice became a national bestseller. The first 39 pages of the book tell of his introspection and provide the above quotations. The majority of the book provides a black man's analysis of racism in

America. It is filled with hatred for "everything American – including baseball and hot dogs."

After his parole from prison, Cleaver co-founded the radical Black Panther movement. He declared war on America, advocating urban guerilla warfare. He led an ambush on Oakland police officers during which two officers were wounded. He was a wanted man by the FBI. He became an enthusiastic supporter of Marxism and Communism. With his re-arrest imminent, he jumped a $50,000 bail and fled into exile.

In exile, Cleaver wanted to build up his forces from abroad and experience the superiority of Communism first-hand. He visited Cuba, North Korea, China, the Soviet Union, and Algeria. While travelling, Eldridge Cleaver had two primary issues to resolve. The first was political. But rather than enhance his view of Communism, his visits to communist countries had the opposite effect. He became disillusioned.

> To go to a country like Cuba or Algeria or the Soviet Union and see the nature of control that those state apparatuses had over the people—it was shocking to me. I didn't want to believe it, because it meant that the politics that I was espousing was wrong. . . . I had heard so much rhetoric about their glorious leaders and their incredible revolutionary spirit that even to this very angry and disgruntled American, it was absurd and unreal. . . . With all its faults, the American political system is the freest and most democratic in the world. . . . I used to be a Marxist and I used to think all our problems were economic and political. But at the end of the day I found out that our main problems are spiritual problems.[6]

And so, the second issue for Eldridge Cleaver to resolve was spiritual. The first epiphany that would change his life was becoming a father.

The most powerful, single breakthrough, in my Communist-held position, was the birth of my children. For me, each one was sort of a cosmic, spiritual event . . . a miracle. . . . [In communism], music, poetry, your soul, and everything that is related to religion was false. I had seen now in my own experience with my children that this was not true. My own experience as a parent was basically enough philosophy to instruct me that there was a Supreme Being, with or without Karl Marx's endorsement.[7]

That was the beginning. But, spiritually he was still alone and despondent. After five years in exile, the family moved to France and lived underground. The luster of his Marxism pursuit had faded and he was an outcast from his own country. He contemplated suicide and one night had his gun in his hand. Alone on a Mediterranean night in France, gazing at the moon, Cleaver had what he described as a vision.

I saw my former heroes paraded before my eyes. Here were Fidel Castro, Mao Tse-tung, Karl Marx, Frederick Engels, passing in review – each one appearing for a moment of time, and then dropping out of sight, like fallen heroes. Finally, at the end of the procession, in dazzling shimmering light, the image of Jesus Christ appeared.[8]

Cleaver crumbled to his knees and sobbed. It was his pivot point.

Eldridge Cleaver contemplated his dilemma. Outside America was not home – he was a foreigner. Inside America he was a fugitive who had broken parole and was still charged with attempted murder. Yet, he found there was only one resolution. After an absence of almost eight years, he arranged a deal with the United States government and returned to the U.S. under guard of two FBI agents. He had made the statement, "There was nothing in life that I hated more than a prison." Yet Cleaver returned to America knowing he would be arrested and incarcerated.

He pled guilty to the assault charge associated with the police shootout. He was confined to the Alameda County Jail for 8 months. This time it was different. Behind bars, Cleaver again wrote, but this time the book was not *Soul on Ice*, but *Soul on Fire*. The books are as different as the titles. In Soul on Fire he describes the transformation, aliveness and exhilaration of his soul. Cleaver made his prison time sound like a religious retreat.

> I was not in prison . . . . Something else was going on.
> I was passing through prison; I was in prison but not in
> prison. . . . As I began crying tears of joy, God then be-
> gan unraveling the mess. . . . The Lord has transported
> me from worldly revolutions to a radical dependence on
> his transforming power.[9]

Charges of attempted murder were dropped and Cleaver was released from jail with the sentence of performing 1,200 hours of community service.

His spiritual inclinations led Cleaver to investigate a number of organized religions. In the process, he became an advocate for what he called "Christlam" – a fusion of Christianity and Islam. He spoke at more than fifty university campuses and at scores of churches and service clubs. In 1983, he was baptized a member of the Mormon Church (Church of Jesus Christ of Latter-day Saints). For a time, he was partially active in church activities and periodically was asked to speak.

The other radical change for Cleaver was political. As stated, he became a "born-again" Republican. He joined the Republican Party in the early 1980s and made several runs for political office. He had earlier written, "I used to really plan on how to kill Ronald Reagan. I'm talking about hatred, hatred that was blind to any other influence. I don't have that hatred any more." In 1984, Cleaver ended up giving speeches for the re-election of Ronald Reagan.[10]

Eldridge Cleaver died in 1998 at the age of 62. He was a complex man and consistency was sometimes lacking. Even with the transformation which had taken place in his life, Cleaver continued to have struggles related to marriage fidelity, drugs, and even the law. His family was broken as Kathleen, his wife, filed for divorce. Nonetheless, he still maintained convictions of democracy, a supreme being, and a divine spark within man.

> [There is] a tiny spark hidden somewhere inside you which cannot die, which even you cannot kill or quench and which tortures you horribly because all the odds are against its continual burning. In the midst of the foulest decay and putrid savagery, this spark speaks to you of beauty, of human warmth and kindness, of goodness, of greatness, of heroism, of martyrdom, and it speaks to you of love.[11]

QUESTIONS TO PONDER AND DISCUSS:

1. After he thought about his crimes of rape, it wasn't the law that became a deterrent. What was it and what are the implications?

2. What does Cleaver's statement mean, "I was passing through prison; I was in prison but not in prison."

3. In your opinion, what are the most basic reasons for Eldridge Cleaver's drastic change?

A QUESTION FOR A WRITTEN ANSWER:

What is the one lesson for you to remember from Eldridge Cleaver?

"The story of my experiments with truth"

17
Mohandas K. Gandhi
1869 – 1948

As a young man, Mohandas K. Gandhi acknowledged, "I was a coward." Yet he confronted the might of Great Britain and led India to independence. In the process, he was arrested several times and spent a total of more than six years in jail. It was there he began to write, noting, "I simply want to tell the story of my numerous experiments with truth . . . my life consists of nothing but those experiments." This message is reinforced in the sub-title of his book: *Gandhi An Autobiography, The Story of My Experiments with Truth.*[1]

EARLY LIFE

His early life gave no hint of later achievement. Along with acknowledging he was a coward, he added,

> I certainly looked feeble-bodied . . . . I did not dare to
> stir out of doors at night. Darkness was a terror to me.
> It was almost impossible for me to sleep in the dark,
> as I would imagine ghosts coming from one direction,
> thieves from another and serpents from a third. . . . I
> could not therefore bear to sleep without a light in the

room. How could I disclose my fears to my wife? . . .
I knew that she had more courage than I, and I felt
ashamed of myself.[2]

Speaking of his wife, through parental arrangement, he was married at age thirteen.

Gandhi began to be driven by his "experiments with truth." While attending law school in London, there was no money for transportation. So, he walked eight or ten miles a day. He concluded, "It was mainly this habit of long walks that kept me practically free from illness throughout my stay in England and gave me a fairly strong body."

His diet was meager as he switched from sweets to foods such as boiled spinach. He concluded, "Such experiments taught me that the real seat of taste was not the tongue but the mind." He later came to the conclusion that his diet should consist of nothing but sun-baked fruits and nuts.

Gandhi obtained his law degree from the University College London, but he was still excruciatingly shy. He prepared a speech for a professional meeting but was too afraid to stand in front of an audience and read it. He had to have someone else do that for him. The first time he presented a case in small claims court, "I stood up, but my heart sank into my boots. My head was reeling and I felt as though the whole court was doing likewise. I could think of no question to ask. The judge must have laughed, and the [other attorneys] no doubt enjoyed the spectacle."[3] Because he was too shy to speak in court, his attempt to establish a law practice in Bombay failed.

This is the man who stood up to the power and domination of Great Britain – and won. How did this happen?

SOUTH AFRICA

Gandhi accepted a job in South Africa. On the way there, this "man of color" was thrown off the train after refusing to move from first-class. On a stagecoach, he refused to move to make room for a European passenger and was beaten by the driver. He was barred from staying in several hotels. Seeing degradation heaped upon himself and his countrymen became a turning point in Gandhi's life. He was awakened by social injustice. He realized his calling was to organize the Indian people in South Africa to achieve a better life. The original plan was to stay in South Africa one year. Working for social justice caused him to stay an additional twenty years.

INDIA

In 1915 he returned home to India. Gandhi's primary goal became the establishment of India's independence from British domination. He became the leader of the movement, adopting the central principle of non-violence. His method was mass civil disobedience and peaceful non-cooperation with the British government. This caused the country to become unmanageable for the British. India achieved freedom August 15, 1947 without resorting to violence.

GANDHI'S MENTORS

Mohandas K. Gandhi was given the honorific title of "Mahatma," meaning "Great Soul." It became customary to address him as Mahatma Gandhi. He inspired tens of millions of people, not only in India but around the world. Where did Gandhi turn for his own inspiration?

> But in all my trials of a spiritual nature, as a lawyer, in conducting institutions, and in politics, I can say that God saved me. When every hope is gone, when helpers fail and comforts flee, I find that help arrives somehow, from I know not where. Supplication, worship, prayer are not superstition.[4]

Through reading, Gandhi found mentors in jail. "Most of my reading since 1893 has been done in jail." Following are books of influence.

Leo Tolstoy: *The Kingdom of God is Within You* – "[It] overwhelmed me. It left an abiding impression on me."

John Ruskin: *Unto This Last* – "I determined to change my life in accordance with the ideals of the book."

Henry David Thoreau: An essay On the Duty of Civil Disobedience – "[His] ideas influenced me greatly . . . . I actually took the name of my movement from Thoreau's essay."

The Bhagavad-Gita: – "When doubts haunt me, when disappointments stare me in the face, and I see not one ray of hope on the horizon, I turn to the *Bhagavad-Gita* and find a verse to comfort me; and I immediately begin to smile in the midst of overwhelming sorrow."

SPIRITUALITY - SERVICE

Gandhi said his spiritual orientation led him to dedicate himself to a life of service.

> We are all tarred with the same brush, and are children of one and the same Creator, and as such the divine powers within us are infinite. To slight a single human being is to slight those divine powers, and thus to harm not only that being but with him the whole world. . . . It is no exaggeration, but the literal truth, to say that in this meeting with the peasants I was face to face with God.[5]

INTEGRITY

Gandhi was not a powerful speaker; he would rather *do* than talk. But the people wanted to hear him. One day as he was leaving Calcutta on the train, the crowd pressed him to give them a message. His statement was simple and profound, "My life is my message."

AN UNTIMELY END

In India there was tension between the Hindus and Muslims. January 30, 1948 at age 78, Mohandas K. Gandhi was assassinated. Gandhi was Hindu, his assassin was also Hindu but disagreed with

Gandhi's doctrine of nonviolence and thought Gandhi was too sympathetic to India's Muslims. Upon his death, Prime Minister Nehru addressed the nation through radio saying, "The light has gone out of our lives." Gandhi's wife had died during one of his imprisonments. He had four children.

An American journalist wrote what could be the ultimate acknowledgement: "This small man, so full of a large love of men, extended beyond India and beyond time … There was a mirror in the Mahatma in which everyone could see the best in himself."

THE INFLUENCE OF MAHATMA GANDHI

Gandhi's influence may have accelerated even after his death. Here is a sample of his legacy.

Dr. Martin Luther King said, "Gandhi was the guiding light of our technique of nonviolent social change."

The Dalai Lama wrote, "His life has inspired me ever since I was a small boy."

Nelson Mandela referred to Gandhi as "the sacred warrior . . . . [He] combined ethics and morality with a steely resolve . . . . Gandhi's message of peace and non-violence holds the key to human survival in the 21st century."

Barack Obama was asked who he would most like to have dinner with. His quick reply was, "Gandhi. He's somebody I find a lot of inspiration in."

Albert Einstein exchanged letters with Gandhi and called him "A role model for the generations to come . . . [who] will scarce believe that such a one as this walked the earth in flesh and blood."

QUESTIONS TO PONDER AND DISCUSS:

1. What does the statement mean, "There was a mirror in the Mahatma in which everyone could see the best in himself?"

2. Comment on the meaning of Gandhi's statement, "My life is my message."

3. What does it mean that Gandhi's life was the story of his "experiments with truth"?

A QUESTION FOR A WRITTEN ANSWER:

What is the one lesson for you to remember from Mahatma Gandhi?

18

Ten Lessons from the Mentors

You have met sixteen men and women who have experienced incarceration, dealt with the mind-forged manacles, and achieved extraordinary personal advancement. While our mentors are a diverse lot, there is remarkable similarity in the prison lessons they mastered and the values they clarified. This chapter identifies ten lessons from the mentors.

VALUE OF CONFINEMENT

It was common for the mentors to acknowledge significant personal growth related to the adversity of prison, though not all made such extraordinary statements as the following.

Bill Dallas: "Doing time in San Quentin was by far the hardest thing I have ever done. But it was also the best thing that ever happened to me, and I would not trade a single minute of that ordeal. . . . I discovered the principles that would eventually enable me to live a meaningful and successful life."

Alexandr Solzhenitsyn: "I turn back to the years of my imprisonment and say, sometimes to the astonishment of those about me: 'Bless you, prison!' . . . I nourished my soul there, and I say without hesitation: 'Bless you, prison, for having been in my life!'"

VALUE OF SIMPLICITY

Because of the stark conditions of prison life, a person might expect the primary response of our mentors to be significantly negative. Typically, this was not the case. Instead, there was an appreciation for simplicity (this seems to apply less to those prisoners of war who suffered severe deprivation).

Dietrich Bonhoeffer: "Prison life in general brings one back, both outwardly and inwardly, to the simplest things of life . . . . The last two years have taught me how little we can get along with."

Bill Dallas: "I was astonished to discover how little I really required to live a contented, if seemingly Spartan, life . . . I learned to find contentment in the simple things."

Anwar Sadat: "The ties which had bound me to the material world began to be severed, one after another. My soul, having jettisoned its earthly freight, was freed and so took off like a bird soaring into space, into the furthest regions of existence, into infinity."

VALUE OF LEARNING

Some of our mentors were without books and longed for them. A few of these, like James Stockdale, brought a rich educational storehouse with them and were involved in "mining the memory." Others, at least at times, had some access to books and in these cases devoured them ravenously.

Eldridge Cleaver: "I had evolved a crash program which I would immediately activate whenever I was placed in solitary: stock up on books and read, read, read."

Fyodor Dostoyevsky: "I had not read a single book for several years, and it is hard to describe the strange excitement I felt as I read my first book in prison. I remember that I began to read it one evening, after lock-up, and I went on reading all night, until daybreak."

Nelson Mandela: "Robben Island was known as the university because of what we learned from each other. We became our own faculty, with our own professors, our own curriculum, our own courses."

Anwar Sadat: "I read voraciously, finding in every word a novelty – something that opened up new horizons before my very eyes. . . . When an idea, a poem, or anything in print appealed to me, I immediately copied it into a notebook that I still keep and really cherish."

VALUE OF SELF-EXAMINATION

Many of our mentors acknowledged that the demands of their pre-prison life had crowded out time for self-examination. Prison gave them the opportunity to look within. With more time and purpose than previously available, these mentors conducted a significant personal inventory. They sorted through the clutter to locate their core, their essence.

Anwar Sadat: "Nothing is more important than self-knowledge. Once I had come to know what I wanted, and got rid of what I didn't, I was reconciled to my 'self' and learned to live at peace with it."

Eldridge Cleaver: "After I returned to prison, I took a long look at myself and, for the first time in my life, admitted that I was wrong, that I had gone astray."

Bill Dallas: "A life in slow motion enabled those of us who had suffered from a lack of contemplation to come face-to-face with who we were, who we wanted to be, who we could be."

James Stockdale: "Contemplation during my years in solitary confinement led me to conclude that a good life is one that accumulates high-quality memories . . . memories of bold strokes of service which one knows in his gut really mattered in the course of history."

VALUE OF SOLITUDE

It is probable that the value of solitude is related to the conditions, the length of time involved, and the personal character of the individual. Nonetheless, it was significant that many of our mentors acknowledged the positive benefits of being entirely alone.

Dietrich Bonhoeffer: "I've come to love solitude. . . . I've got so used to the silence of solitude by now that after a short time I long for it again. . . . You need to get right down to fundamentals, to come to terms with life, and for that you need plenty of time to yourself."

Fyodor Dostoyevsky: "I experienced the most terrible isolation and in the end I came to cherish that isolation. Inwardly alone, I reviewed the whole of my past life . . . sometimes even blessed fate for having sent me such isolation."

Anwar Sadat: "In Cell 54 I could only be my own companion, day and night . . . . The only way in which I could break my loneliness was, paradoxically, to seek the companionship of that inner entity I call 'self.'"

James Stockdale: "Isolation seems to have some sort of a purifying effect on the soul."

VALUE OF CHANGE

It has long seemed to me that one of the most fundamental of all questions is this: once a personality is formed, can authentic change take place? Our mentors are surprisingly positive in their answers with an optimistic message that genuine change can take place.

Eldridge Cleaver: "I used to really plan on how to kill . . . . I'm talking about hatred, hatred that was blind to any other influence. I don't have that hatred any more."

Anwar Sadat: "My contemplation of life and human nature in that secluded place had taught me that he who cannot change the very fabric of his thought will never be able to . . . make any progress."

Viktor Frankl: "It becomes clear that the sort of person the prisoner became was the result of an inner decision, and not the result of camp influences alone. Fundamentally, therefore, any man can, even under such circumstances, decide what shall become of him – mentally and spiritually. . . . Every human being has the freedom to change at any instant."

VALUE OF OTHERS

The philosopher Martin Buber pointed out the distinction between the "I – you" relationship as opposed to the "*I – Thou*" relationship. It seems all of our mentors moved toward "I – Thou" relationships.

Mahatma Gandhi: "To slight a single human being is to slight those divine powers. . . . It is no exaggeration, but the literal truth, to say that in this meeting with the peasants I was face to face with God."

Nelson Mandela: "Even in the grimmest times when . . . pushed to our limits, I would see a glimmer of humanity in one of the guards . . . . Man's goodness is a flame that can be hidden but never extinguished."

Corrie ten Boom: [In solitary confinement] "I was as starved for the sight of a human face as for the food." [In taking a shower] "Even in the strict silence this human closeness was joy and strength . . . I thought, they are all my sisters. How rich is anyone who can simply see human faces!"

Alexandr Solzhenitsyn: "That Spring – 1945, I came to understand that it was my duty to take upon my shoulders a share of [my fellow prisoners] common burden – and to bear it to the last man, until it crushed us."

James Stockdale: "And the most important idea, as we strove to maintain our sanity, was this: *You are your brother's keeper.*"

VALUE OF PHYSICAL ACTIVITY

Many of our mentors recognized the value of physical activity in spite of severe space restrictions.

Nelson Mandela: "Rising before dawn at Robben Island: "I would do stationary running in my cell . . . for up to forty-five minutes. I would also perform one hundred fingertip push-ups, two hundred sit-ups, fifty deep knee-bends, and various other calisthenics."

James Stockdale: "Self-discipline was vital to self-respect . . . . I would do 400 pushups a day, even when I had leg irons, and would feel guilty when I failed to do them."

Mahatma Gandhi: Didn't mention exercise during incarceration, but in London with no money available for transportation, he established a life-long habit of walking eight or ten miles a day. "It was mainly this habit of long walks that kept me practically free from illness . . . and gave me a fairly strong body."

Anwar Sadat: When finally allowed out of his cell, "I walked 2-1/2 miles every morning, and still do."

VALUE OF FORGIVENESS

Forgiveness is one of the most dramatic of the lessons incorporated by a large number of our mentors. It is easy to feel our judgments are justified and others deserve our mistreatment. Yet, most of our mentors spoke of forgiveness. They recognized that forgiveness releases the one forgiving.

Alexandr Solzhenitsyn: "Formerly you never forgave anyone. You judged people without mercy. . . . And now, you have come to realize your own weakness – and you can therefore understand the weakness of others."

Corrie ten Boom: Writing to the informant who caused her and her family to be arrested, "I went through 10 months of concentration camp. My father died after 9 days. . . . My sister died in prison, too. . . . I came nearer to [God] . . . I have forgiven you everything."

Bill Dallas: "Forgiveness was the final, critical key to my own personal transformation. . . . to be truly free, I still needed to deal with the unresolved anger in my heart . . . . When we extend forgiveness to the one who has hurt us . . . the prize is our own freedom."

Louis Zamperini: "I believed hating was the same as getting even. . . . All I did was destroy myself with my hate. [To 'the Bird'] . . . love replaced the hate I had for you. . . . Like the others, I also forgave you."

VALUE OF SPIRITUALITY

Prisons are sometimes viewed as dens of iniquity. As I studied these mentors, I was surprised to learn that, almost to a person, a divine spark was mentioned and a dominant theme was spirituality. I was reminded of Blaise Pascal, the French philosopher and mathematician who concluded, "There is a God-shaped vacuum in the heart of every man."

Eldridge Cleaver: "The Lord has transported me from worldly revolutions to a radical dependence on his transforming power. . . . [There is] a tiny spark hidden somewhere inside you which cannot die."

Boethius: [Lady Wisdom] ". . . men become happy by acquiring divinity."

Louis Zamperini: "The post-war nightmares caused my life to crumble, but thanks to a confrontation with God . . . I committed my life to Christ."

Mahatma Gandhi: "But in all my trials . . . I can say that God saved me. When every hope is gone, when helpers fail and comforts flee, I find that help arrives somehow, from I know not where."

19
The Lessons: Personal Application

Now the question is: *so what*? What about everyday prisoner # 999999 evaluating his or her life? What about the man or woman on the street experimenting with introspection? What about *you*? Are *your* life-lessons similar to those of our prison mentors?

In examining my own life, I have been intrigued to discover I have been, and am still, involved in learning the same lessons as the mentors. I find I call on the inspiration of these prison mentors regularly. I hesitated to add another chapter to this book describing my personal experience with the lessons. However, I respond to encouragement to do so. I have found the lessons and values of the mentors are at the core of who I am. I share my experiences with the ten lessons in hope they may be of value in your own considerations, your own "ascending" (to use the word of Alexandr Solzhenitsyn).

VALUE OF CONFINEMENT (ADVERSITY)

Early in my life, I had a feeling there must be something more. As a youngster at home, I didn't learn much about relationships, communicating, or thriving. A feeling of isolation was my prison. In college I gained a broader view of life, others and self, and became aware of my own constraint. And with that recognition, I found a benefit – it accelerated introspection, curiosity, and exploration.

A friend and I decided the best way to make up for lost time was to go travelling around the world. I dropped out of college for a year, worked a construction job for three months, and saved. We hitchhiked to Los Angeles and caught a flight to Hawaii. In Hawaii, I drove a taxicab and most nights hauled drunk sailors from Hotel Street to Pearl Harbor. We booked passage on a British ship with stops in Japan, Hong Kong, Manila, Singapore, Bombay, Saudi Arabia, and Egypt. In Italy, we bought an old, beat-up Volkswagen and spent most nights sleeping in the car throughout Europe and the Soviet Union. Our typical menu was bread, cheese, and jam. After a year, we arrived in New York with $13 each, bought a short bus ride out of the city, and hitchhiked home to Utah.

For most of a year we were drenched in freedom – where to go, what to see, what to think. I traded narrowness for expansiveness. I learned to value people different from me and found they were not as different as I had thought. I learned self-reliance and the capacity to function far outside my comfort zone. I gained an appreciation for the opportunities in America. I learned that a spiritual dimension is central to who I am. I found my confinement had launched me into a huge, new world.

THE VALUE OF SIMPLICITY

One of the issues I have had to deal with is, how much is enough? I am inundated with the message of *more, bigger, and better* – more stuff, a bigger house, a newer car, toys galore. A modest income has kept in check most of the craving for *more*. However, I had another advantage – I had the good fortune of spending a significant part of my teen years on a farm in Gusher, Utah (don't even try to find it on a map). Mostly we were without electricity or running water, we kept warm around a coal stove and read with a kerosene lantern. I learned how to plough with a team of horses and put 81 little piglets into boxes behind the kitchen stove so they wouldn't freeze in the below-zero winter. I learned what was essential and what was excess. If Henry David Thoreau would have had kids, I would have been one of them.

I just completed a jettison-the-junk project. My room, my closets, my garage were full of *stuff*. It made most everything difficult to find. It not only cluttered my world, but my mind. I can't afford a bigger house to store my *stuff*, so that left me with getting rid of *stuff*. If I hadn't used something in a year, its tenure was in jeopardy. If I hadn't used it in two years, it was gone. What I kept is organized and labeled. Amazingly, my premises went from cramped to spacious.

Dietrich Bonhoeffer mentioned an *inner* simplicity. To me that involves an assessment of my inner furnishings. It involves discarding agitation, fearfulness, and things I can do nothing about. It is keeping those things that contribute to peace and abundance.

VALUE OF LEARNING

Our mentors voiced excitement over books. With embarrassment, I acknowledge my early delinquency with books. On a summer day in the middle of a Master's degree program, I was sitting in front of a campus fountain. As I watched the cascading water, I contemplated the status of my life and felt dissatisfaction. And then I came to a startling realization. Since childhood I could not recall reading one book that was not required for a class – not one! Further, I realized that was indicative of my life – only doing what was assigned, meeting the expectations of others, not exploring or challenging or searching for myself. I was incarcerated in a tiny, tiny world.

That very day I stopped by the university library and visited a foreign floor where fiction was housed. I was almost surprised to find my library card worked as well for a Jack London book as one written by Abraham Maslow. The next few months I read twenty-two non-school books. I read history and novels, but my favorites were biographies and autobiographies.

When I tasted the freedom of books, they became as oxygen. I can live dozens of lives; I can play with hundreds of ideas. Most of my books I check out from the public library. Sometimes I start a book from the library, realize it is a keeper, and buy a used copy online. In addition, there are thousands of books I can download free on my Kindle. If a meeting is boring, out comes my Kindle (it is amazing how much reading is accomplished that way). My ideal summer job would be as a fire watch on a tower in Oregon with a truckload of books. I think I would start with Will and Ariel Durant's eleven volume history – *The Story of Civilization*.[1]

VALUE OF SELF- EXAMINATION

I remember a particularly crucial time in my life that demanded introspection. A quarter-century ago I had a tumor removed from my shoulder which was diagnosed as carcinoma. It was a secondary site that had spread from an unknown primary source. After extensive testing, I questioned the doctor. "What is the best scenario?" He answered, "They will find the source of the cancer, treat it with radiation and cure you – which is unlikely." "And, what is the worst scenario, doctor?" "Death within a few months. The probability is something between."

This jump-started an extensive life review. Though progress had been made, I was still a beginner using a small part of my capacity. While I had limited satisfaction from my job, I did have an extraordinarily supportive wife. And marvel of marvels, after so many years, I had a two-year-old daughter. I was finally a daddy! More than anything, I wanted to be there for my little girl. I recommitted to exercise, healthy eating, and life.

After more than twenty-five years, the primary source of the cancer has never surfaced. At this writing, I am seventy-seven years old. To celebrate my seventieth birthday, I did seventy pushups and went skydiving. With a trusting wife, we had another daughter. I am now a grandfather, working for educational opportunities for prisoners, helping in the family business, and still adding new challenges.

VALUE OF SOLITUDE

I seem to be a maverick. I enjoy significant conversations, particularly one-on-one or in small groups. However, I can pass on most large gatherings. I like alone time and appreciated the discovery that many of our mentors found value in solitude.

Here is one of my rituals. I had been to Utah's High Uinta Mountains as a Boy Scout. Many years later, when I was confronted with a difficult decision, the mountain called. Alone with backpack and tent, I made my way up the steep and rocky trail to a lake I had remembered as a boy. Alone I grappled with my circumstance and my demons. Four days later I hiked down the mountain, but I was not alone. My companions were clarity, resolve, and courage.

While my mountain retreat had served me well, I felt I would not be returning. Yet, when the next August came, though there was not the urgency, the mountain again beckoned and I retraced my steps to my mountain lake. The years merged into decades, and as the swallows return to Capistrano, for thirty-eight years I have returned to my lake for my solo appointment. It is a time of immersion in the supreme peace, splendor and tranquility of nature. It is a time to release disappointment and celebrate victory. It is a time to deepen gratitude, recommit to love, and reestablish contact with essence. It is a time to rediscover God's hiding place – and find it is deep within my soul. It is a time to realign with the Light. These are days that have become vital to my soul.

VALUE OF CHANGE

When interviewed by Oprah Winfrey in 2001, Nelson Mandela said: "If I had not been in prison, I would not have been able to achieve the most difficult task in life, and that is changing yourself." Change is difficult, but our mentors seem to agree it is possible. Perhaps the key is found in an old Hebrew proverb: "Change takes but an instant. It's the resistance to change that can take a lifetime."

Probably my most significant change has involved my religious perspective. Somehow as a youth, it seems I picked up the wrong emphasis. The religious message I heard was one of punishment and reward. Coupled with it was the message of duty, responsibility, ought, supposed to, and should. If I did what I was *supposed* to, I would be rewarded with good things in the next life. If I failed to do my *duty*, I would be punished in the next life with bad things. It seemed a lot like our school grading system, earning the "A" or the "F."

But the more I studied and thought, the more I decided my perspective was wrong. I concluded the moral, ethical life is to be lived because, at my depth, there is divinity and godliness. It is who I am – my integrity demands it. My challenge is to activate that godliness to the benefit of my fellow-travelers. Further, I believe in the goodness of others – that all have a divine spark that cannot be extinguished. I am to recognize that spark and contribute to its igniting. Sometimes I do better than other times. I was compelled to write my conclusions in a book, *Beside Still Waters – 52 Reflections of the Divine Within*.[2]

VALUE OF OTHERS

In my study of the New Testament, I identify with a man who had been partially healed by Jesus. When asked what he saw, he replied, "I see men as trees, walking." Sometimes I am that way – partially healed, seeing men and women as *things* walking. When Jesus fully healed the man, he reported a very different experience, he "saw every man clearly."[3] I know I am healed when I see each person clearly – their discouragements and unmet dreams, their possibilities and magnificence.

I have a routine I am beginning to include in my meditation and at random times during the day: I send a *light-zing*. It is a beam of light that resembles a soft and gentle stream of lightning. I don't know that anyone feels it, but I know that after I have sent a *light-zing* to someone, I treat them with greater patience and kindness.

One of my slow starts was in relationships. I was forty-seven years old when I married my wife Susie and inherited three marvelous children. I didn't do everything right, but I think during the next couple of years I learned more about giving than any other kid on the block. And then we had two new, magnificent additions to the family. So, after decades of being an introverted bachelor, I began learning to love and give and now count this family, which has grown to the number twenty-one, to be my greatest asset and my most important teacher.

VALUE OF PHYSICAL ACTIVITY

As a kid, I wanted to play football but found I wasn't adept enough or rugged enough. However, more than fifty years ago when I was discharged from active military duty, I was in good physical condition. When I got home, I made one of the best decisions of my life – I decided to stay in shape. For more than fifty years I have been on a gym and jog program (I used to call it running – next it will be ambling). For me, random scheduling doesn't work. I have to make an appointment with myself and have concluded these self-appointments are my most important appointments to keep. Three times a week I do my gym and jog routine. I max out on fruits and veggies (I haven't yet given up ice cream but I do fifty pushups most days to make up for it). When the gym scales register more than 155 pounds, I cut back on my eating. I have a goal to live to be a hundred. I think I will make it for there is much left to do. I like George Burns' statement, "I want to die young – at a ripe old age."

VALUE OF FORGIVENESS

I found it significant the number of our prison mentors who discovered that forgiveness was critical in their transformation process. Personally, I don't remember huge wrongs inflicted upon me. However, in a general way, I have had a feeling of being a victim of circumstance. I could have gotten a better roll of the dice – a more encouraging home life, more assertiveness, more athleticism, more sociability, more playfulness. I have found the following three conclusions helpful.

1. *What is, is.* I am not in charge of the universe or God or others, and I am to come to peace with the way things are. I have smiled at Robert Frost's observation: "Forgive, O Lord, my little jokes on Thee, and I'll forgive Thy great big joke on me."

2. *People are doing the best they can with what they have.* The words of Total Quality Management guru, W. Edwards Deming, have been a guide to me, "Don't fix the blame, fix the problem."

3. *Don't be offended.* It has been decades since I have been offended. It makes life much easier.

VALUE OF SPIRITUALITY

You have noticed a dominant theme of spirituality in the writings of our mentors as well as my own comments. I was raised in a religiously orthodox Utah home and served as a missionary for my church. While still adhering to the faith of my fathers (and mothers), I have been drawn to explore my own spiritual path on an expansive and marvelous journey. I have arrived at five core principles.

• There is a Divine Creator who has implanted godliness at the center of each person.

• Jesus is my exemplar – following His way brings peace and accelerated living.

• My needs are simple, the gifts are great – I live in peace, joy, gratitude, and awe.

• I have enough – my mission is to give.

• I am a beginner and a seeker; I am evolving and ascending.

~ ~ ~ ~ ~

And so we finish the journey we began. I leave you with one last thought from one of my own mentors, Louis L'Amour. "There will come a time when you believe everything is finished. Yet that will be the beginning."

And so it is – a beginning. A life filled with mentors is different from a life alone. You have met mentors who, as you invite them, are eager to become your advocates. As you read more of their writings, there is much more they have to teach. And beyond that, there are unlimited additional mentors with a special invitation – for you.

THE BEGINNING

20
References

1. Mind-Forged Manacles

1. *Songs of Innocence and of Experience*, "London," William Blake, 1794.
2. *Mathematical Circles Adieu*, H. Eves, 1977, Albert Einstein letter dated 1950.
3. *The Creative Process*, Brewster Ghiselin, A Mentor Book, Univ. of California Press, 1955, p. 13.
4. *Holy Bible*, King James version, Psalms 142:7.
5. *To Lucasta*, "To Althea from Prison," Richard Lovelace, written in 1642, published in 1649.

2. Nelson Mandela

1. *Long Walk to Freedom*, Nelson Mandela, Little, Brown and Co., 1994.
2. Ibid, p. 389.
3. Ibid, pp. 385-86.
4. Ibid, p. 491.
5. Ibid, p. 622.
6. Ibid, p. 622.
7. Ibid, Chapter 9.
8. Ibid, p. 624.

9. Playing the Enemy – the Game That Made a Nation, Nelson Mandela and John Carlin, The Penguin Press, New York, 2008, p. 151.

10. *Playing the Enemy*, Ibid.

11. *Long Walk to Freedom*, Ibid, p. 625.

3. Bill Dallas

1. *Lessons from San Quentin, Everything I Needed to Know about Life I Learned in Prison*, Bill Dallas, Tyndale House Publishers, Inc., Carol Stream, Illinois, 2009.

2. Ibid, pp. 182-83.

3. Ibid, pp. 35-36.

4. Ibid, p. xxiii.

5. Ibid, pp. 151-52.

6. Ibid, pp. 154, 157.

7. Ibid, pp. 91-93.

8. Ibid, p. 43.

9. Ibid, p. 59.

10. Ibid, pp. 61,107.

11. Ibid, pp. xixi, 7-8.

12. Ibid, p. 60.

13. Ibid, p. 9.

14. Ibid, p. 21.

15. Ibid, p. 164.

16. Ibid, pp. 189-90.

17. Ibid, p. 171.

18. Ibid, pp. xx.

19. Ibid, pp. 121-22.

4. Louis Zamperini

1. *Devil at My Heels*, Louis Zamperini & David Rensin, Harper, New York, 2003.

2. *Unbroken, A World War II Story of Survival, Resilience, and Redemption*, Laura Hillenbrand, Random House, New York, 2010.

3. *Devil at My Heels*, Ibid, p. 96.

4. *Devil at My Heels*, Ibid, p. 106.

5. *Devil at My Heels*, Ibid, p. 93.

6. *Devil at My Heels*, Ibid, p. 99.

7. *Devil at My Heels*, Ibid, pp. 176-178.

8. *Unbroken*, Ibid, p. 315.

9. *Unbroken*, Ibid, p. 367.

10. *Devil at My Heels*, Ibid, pp. 232-233, 236.

11. *Devil at My Heels*, Ibid, pp. 242-245.

12. *Unbroken*, Ibid, p. 397.

5. Corrie Ten Boom

1. *The Hiding Place*, Corrie ten Boom, Chosen Books, 25th Anniversary Edition, Grand Rapids, Michigan, 1971.

2. *Prison Letters*, Corrie ten Boom, Fleming H. Revell Company, Old Tappan, New Jersey, 1975.

3. *The Hiding Place*, Ibid, pp. 138,140.

4. *The Hiding Place*, Ibid, p. 144.

5. *Prison Letters*, Ibid, pp. 18, 21, 28.

6. *The Hiding Place*, Ibid, p. 161.

7. *The Hiding Place*, Ibid, p. 165.

8. *The Hiding Place*, Ibid, pp. 177-178.

9. *The Hiding Place*, Ibid, p. 183.

10. *The Hiding Place*, Ibid, p. 187.

11. *The Hiding Place*, Ibid, pp. 196-197.

12. *Prison Letters*, Ibid, p. 81.

13. *The Hiding Place*, Ibid, pp. 215-216.

14. *The Art of Forgiving*, Lewis B. Smedes, Random House, Inc., 1996, p. 178.

6. Viktor Frankl

1. *Man's Search for Meaning*, Viktor E. Frankl, Simon and Schuster, New York, 1959.
2. Ibid, pp. 9-31.
3. Ibid, p. 82.
4. Ibid, p. 39.
5. Ibid, p. 104.
6. Ibid, pp. 105-106.
7. Ibid, p. 65.
8. Ibid, p. 66.
9. Ibid, p. 65.
10. Ibid, pp. 36-37.
11. Ibid, p. 35.
12. Ibid, p. 32.
13. Ibid, p. 77.
14. Ibid, p. 131.
15. Ibid, pp. 87-90.

7. Alexandr Solzhenitsyn

1. *One Day in the Life of Ivan Denisovich*, Alexandr Solzhenitsyn, translated by Max Hayward and Ronald Hingley, Bantam Classic, 1963.
2. Ibid, p. 21.
3. Ibid, p. 31.
4. Ibid, p. 141.
5. *The Gulag Archipelago*, Alexandr Solzhenitsyn, Harperperennial, New York, 2002.
6. Ibid, p. 98.
7. Ibid, p. 299.
8. Ibid, p. 308.
9. Ibid, p. 309.
10. Ibid, p. 355.
11. Ibid, p. 311.
12. Ibid, p. 305.

13. Ibid, pp. 305-306.
14. Ibid, pp. 308-09.
15. Ibid, p. 357.
16. Ibid, p. 309.
17. Ibid, p. 448.
18. Ibid, pp. 355-56.
19. Ibid, pp. 356-57.
20. Ibid, p. 313.

8. James Stockdale

1. *A Vietnam Experience – Ten Years of Reflection*, James B. Stockdale, Hoover Institution, Stanford University, 1984, p. 89.
2. *Stockdale on Stoicism II: Master of My Fate*, Center for The Study of Professional Military Ethics, http://www.usna.edu/Ethics/publications/documents/Stoicism2.pdf.
3. *Stockdale on Stoicism I: The Stoic Warrior's Triad*, Center for The Study of Professional Military Ethics, http://www.usna.edu/Ethics/publications/documents/stoicism1.pdf.
4. *The Handbook* also called *The Enchiridion*, translated by Nicholas P. White, Hackett Publishing Co., Indianapolis/Cambridge, 1983.
5. *A Vietnam Experience*, Ibid, p. 124.
6. *A Vietnam Experience*, Ibid, p. 110.
7. *A Vietnam Experience*, Ibid, p. 10.
8. *The Handbook*, Ibid, p. 11.
9. *A Vietnam Experience*, Ibid pp. 10, 94.
10. *The Golden Sayings of Epictetus* (a free online EBook Project Gutenberg), pp. 153, 348).
11. *A Vietnam Experience*, Ibid, p. 74.
12. *The Golden Sayings of Epictetus*, Ibid, p. 244.
13. *A Vietnam Experience*, Ibid, p. 107.
14. *A Vietnam Experience*, Ibid, p. 94.
15. *The Golden Sayings of Epictetus*, Ibid, p. 224.
16. *A Vietnam Experience*, Ibid, pp 9, 32.

17. *A Vietnam Experience*, Ibid, p. 119.

18. *In Love and War: The Story of a Family's Ordeal and Sacrifice During the Vietnam War*, James Stockdale and Sybil Stockdale, Naval Institute Press, 1990.

An additional reference: *Courage Under Fire, Testing Epictetus's Doctrines in a Laboratory of Human Behavior*, James Bond Stockdale, Hoover Institution on War, Revolution & Peace, Stanford University, 1993. This is a small, summary book in which Stockdale tells about his association with Epictetus.

9. Fyodor Dostoyevsky

1. *House of the Dead*, Fyodor Dostoyevsky, translated by David McDuff, Penguin Books, 1985, Introduction.

2. *House of the Dead*, Ibid.

3. Ibid, p. 353.

4. Ibid, Translator's Introduction.

5. Ibid, p. 340.

6. Ibid, p. 340.

7. *Crime and Punishment*, Fyodor Dostoevsky, Bantam Classic, New York, 2003.

8. *The Brothers Karamazov*, Fyodor Dostoyevsky, Constance Garnett translator, The Lowell Press, New York, 2009.

9. *The Brothers Karamazov*, Ibid, p. 31

10. *The Brothers Karamazov*, Ibid, pp. 468-69

11. *The Brothers Karamazov*, Fyodor Dostoevsky, The Project Gutenberg EBook, 2009.

10. Joan of Arc

1. *Personal Recollections of Joan of Arc*, Mark Twain, Dover Publications, Inc., Mineola, N.Y., 2002.

2. Ibid, pp. 38, 40.

3. Ibid, p. 42.

4. Ibid, pp. 51-52.

5. Ibid, p. 97.

6. Ibid, pp. 98-99.

7. Ibid, p. 180.

8. Ibid, pp. 133, 135, 205.

9. Ibid, p. 176.

10. Ibid, pp. 213-14.

11. Ibid, pp. 322-23.

12. Ibid, pp. 240, 288, 290.

13. Ibid, p. 299.

14. Ibid, p. 311.

15. Ibid, p. 452.

Note: A trial manuscript is found in *The Trial of Joan of Arc*, W.P. Barrett Gotham House Inc., 1932

11. Anwar Sadat

1. *In Search of Identity, An Autobiography*, Anwar el-Sadat, Harper & Row Publishers, N.Y., 1977.

2. Ibid, p. 8.

3. Ibid, p. 11.

4. Ibid, p. 43.

5. Ibid, pp. 73, 75, 80.

6. Ibid, pp. 76-77.

7. Ibid, pp. 77-79, 86.

8. Ibid, pp. 77-79, 86.

9. Ibid, pp. 76, 88.

10. Ibid, p. 85.

11. Ibid, p. 206.

12. Ibid, p. 303.

13. Ibid, p. 337.

12. Jean Valjean

1. *Les Miserables*, Victor Hugo, Signet, 1987.

2. Ibid, p. 89.

3. Ibid, pp. 87-88.

4. Ibid, pp. 54-55.
5. Ibid, pp. 105-106.
6. Ibid, p. 110.
7. Ibid, pp. 110-111.
8. Ibid, p. 113.
9. Ibid, pp. 160, 162.
10. Ibid, pp. 1460-62.

13. Boethius

1. *The Consolation of Philosophy*, Boethius, Macmillan/Library of Liberal Arts, 1962.
2. Ibid, p. 6.
3. Ibid, pp. 12-14.
4. Ibid, pp. 12-19.
5. Ibid, pp. 21-22, 24.
6. Ibid, pp. 29-32.
7. Ibid, p. 38.
8. Ibid, pp. 40, 42.
9. Ibid, p. 69.
10. Ibid, p. 63.
11. Ibid, pp. 72, 75.

14. Dietrich Bonhoeffer

1. *Letters & Papers from Prison*, Dietrich Bonhoeffer, Macmillan Publishing Co., Inc. New York, 1972.
2. Ibid, p. 3.
3. Ibid, p. 10.
4. Ibid, p. 11.
5. Ibid, p. 39, May 15, 1943.
6. Ibid, p. 272, April 11, 1944.
7. Ibid, p. 333, June 21, 1944.
8. Ibid, p. 50, June 4, 1943.
9. Ibid, p. 401, January 1945.

10. Ibid, p. 53, June 14, 1943.

11. Ibid, p. 178, December 25 Christmas Day.

12. Ibid, p. 271, April 11, 1944.

13. Ibid, p. 297, May, 1944.

14. Ibid, p. 310, May 29, 1944.

15. Ibid, p. 393, August 23, 1944.

16. Ibid, p. 311, May 29, 1944.

17. Ibid, pp. 347-48.

15. Miguel de Cervantes

1. *Don Quixote*, Miguel de Cervantes, translated by John Rutherford, Penguin Books, 2001.

2. *Man of Lamancha*, Dale Wasserman, Joe Darion, Mitch Leigh, Random House, New York, 1966.

3. *Don Quixote*, Ibid.

4. *Man of Lamancha*, Ibid, pp. 77-78.

5. *Man of Lamancha*, Ibid, pp. 78-82 – recognition and thanks to Dale Wasserman, et. al.

16. Eldridge Cleaver

1. *Soul on Ice*, Eldridge Cleaver, A Delta Book, New York, 1968.

2. *Soul on Fire*, Eldridge Cleaver, World Books, Waco Texas, 1978.

3. *Soul on Ice*, Ibid, pp. 4-13.

4. *Soul on Ice*, Ibid, p. 15.

5. *Reason Magazine*, "Interview with Eldridge Cleaver," Lynn Scarlett & Bill Kauffman, Feb., 1986.

6. *Reason Magazine*, Ibid.

7. *Soul on Fire*, Ibid, pp. 134-35.

8. *EarthLight Magazine* #50, "One Journey Home: Eldridge Cleaver's Spiritual Path, Linda Neale, Spring 2004.

9. *Soul on Fire*, Ibid, pages 211-233 for the several quotations.

10. *Reason Magazine*, Ibid.

11. *Wikipedia*, Eldridge Cleaver.

17. Mohandas K. Gandhi

1. *Gandhi An Autobiography, The Story of My Experiments with Truth*, Mohandas K. Gandhi, translated by Mahadev Desai, Beacon Paperback edition, USA, 1957.
2. Ibid, pp. 20-21.
3. Ibid, p. 94.
4. Ibid, p. 72.
5. Ibid, pp. 276, 412.

18. Ten Lessons from the Mentors

19. The Lessons: Personal Application

1. *The Story of Civilization*, Will and Ariel Durant, Simon and Schuster, New York, 1954-1975.
2. *Beside Still Waters – 52 Reflections of the Divine Within*, Donald L. Wright, PivotPoint Books, 2002.
3. *Holy Bible*, King James version, Mark 8:22-25.

20. References

Made in the USA
Middletown, DE
06 January 2018